INSTANT WEIGHT LOSS COOKBOOK 550

550 Quick & Delicious Instant Pot Weight Loss Recipes To Lose Weight

(2021 EDITION)

BY

Kent Chandler

ISBN: 978-1-952504-92-1

COPYRIGHT © 2020 by Kent Chandler

All rights reserved. This book is copyright protected and it's for personal use only. Without the prior written permission of the publisher, no part of this publication should be reproduced, distributed, or transmitted in any form or by any means, including photocopying, recording, or other electronic or mechanical methods.

This publication is sold with the idea that the publisher is not required to render accounting, officially permitted, or otherwise, qualified services. If advice is required, it is necessary to seek the services of a legal or professional, a practiced individual in the profession. This document is geared towards providing substantial and reliable information in regards to the topics covered.

DISCLAIMER

The information written in this book is for educational and entertainment purposes only. Strenuous efforts have been made to provide accurate, up to date and reliable complete information. The information in this book is true and complete to the best of our knowledge. All recommendations are made without guarantee on the part of the author and publisher.

Neither the publisher nor the author takes any responsibility for any possible consequences of reading or enjoying the recipes in this book. The author and publisher disclaim any liability in connection with the use of information contained in this book. Under no circumstance will any legal responsibility or blame be apportioned against the author or publisher for any reparation, damages, or monetary loss due to the information herein, either directly or indirectly.

Table of Contents

INTRODUCTION 7
- Meaning of Instant Pot 7
- Reasons Why You Need An Instant Pot 8
- Functions/Keys Of An Instant Pot 10
- How to Clean Your Instant Pot Effectively 14
- Instant Pot Must-Have Tools 16

BREAKFAST RECIPES 17
- Breakfast Casserole 17
- Egg Muffins 18
- Creamy Taste Pumpkin Maple Oat 19
- Pumpkin Apple Butter 20
- Hard-Boiled Eggs 21
- Pepper Frittata And Broccoli Ham 22
- Regular Oatmeal 23
- Breakfast Quinoa 24
- Buckwheat Porridge 25
- Blueberry Breakfast 26

SOUP, STEW & CHILI RECIPES 27
- Chicken Tortilla Soup 27
- Beef Stew 28
- Stuff Pepper Soup 29
- Turkey Chili 30
- Italian Wedding Soup 31
- Italian Sausage Stew 32
- Beanless Beef Chili 34
- Broccoli Cheese Soup 35
- Loaded Potato And Cauliflower Soup 36
- Sweet Potato Chili 37
- Red Wine Beef Stew 38
- Lemon Chicken Noodle Soup 39
- Chipotle Pumpkin Turkey Chili 41

BEANS, RICE & GRAIN RECIPES 43
- Beans And Rice 43
- 13 Bean Soup 45
- Brown Rice And Beans 46
- Baked Beans 47
- Santa Fe Beans And Rice 48
- Pinto Beans 50
- Refried Beans 51
- Chicken Taco Bowl 52
- Honey Garlic Chicken 53
- Butter Lemon Chicken 54
- Kung Pao Chicken 55
- Orange Chicken 56
- Ground Turkey Lentil Chili 57
- Korean Chicken Meatball 58
- Chicken And Dumplings 59
- Honey Lemon Chicken 60
- Chicken Tortilla-Less Soup 62
- Green Chili Chicken Enchilada Soup 63

BEEF & PORK RECIPES 64
- Beef Stroganoff 64
- Pulled Pork 65
- Mongolian Beef 66
- Spicy Thai Beef Nachos 68
- Boneless Pork Chops 69
- Korean Beef And Brown Rice 70
- Pork Tenderloin Teriyaki 72
- Beef Pot Roast 73
- Smothered Pork Chops 74

FISH & SEAFOOD RECIPES 76
- Steamed Alaskan Crab Legs 76
- Instant Pot Salmon 77

Shrimp Scampi...78

Lemon Pepper Salmon 79

Coconut Fish Curry..80

Sweet And Spicy Pineapple Shrimp 81

Fish Tacos 82

4 Minute Salmon, Broccoli & Potatoes..83

Salmon With Chili-Lime Sauce 84

Savory Shrimp With Tomatoes And Feta 85

Crustless Crab Quiche..86

VEGAN AND VEGETARIAN RECIPES..87

Vegan Butter Chicken with Soy Curls and Chickpeas 87

Maple Bourbon Sweet Potato Chili 89

Easy Vegan Mashed Potatoes 91

Walnut Lentil Tacos...92

Cilantro Lime Quinoa 93

Vegan Lentil Chili 94

Mushroom Risotto 95

Potato Curry...97

Carrot Ginger Soup 98

APPETIZER RECIPES 100

Prosciutto-wrapped Asparagus Canes..100

Black Bean Dip...101

Cocktail Meatballs 102

Buffalo Ranch Chicken Dip 103

Cranberry Pecan Brie 104

Beer-Braised Pulled Ham 105

Mini Teriyaki Turkey Sandwiches 106

Cuban Pulled Pork Sandwiches 107

DESSERT RECIPES 109

Apple Bread with Salted Caramel Icing.. 109

Apple Crisp 110

Mini-Lemon Cheesecakes 111

Berries And Cream Breakfast Cake 113
Apple And Ricotta Cake 115
Applesauce 117
Homemade Pumpkin Puree 118

INTRODUCTION

Meaning of Instant Pot

The Instant Pot Is One Programmable Machine That Does the Work of 7 Gadgets. Instant Pot is a seven-in-one multi-cooker that works as an electric pressure cooker, slow cooker, rice cooker, yogurt maker, steamer, warmer, and sauté pan all in one. Instant Pot is a multi-cooker that offers the same functionalities you'd find in a slow cooker, electric pressure cooker, rice cooker, steamer, yogurt maker, sauté/browning pan, and warming pot. It cooks meals faster, and offers the option for a delayed programmable start time.

The Instant Pot has a lot of functionality for one appliance, and at a decent price point. Most of all, I love the convenience. I can set it and walk away, and it saves time cooking foods like dried beans, lentils, whole grains, and stew. It's also durable and easy to clean. With so much functionality it can feel a little overwhelming and intimidating to learn how to use it. The electric pressure cooker function works at a lower maximum pressure than stovetop pressure cookers (which operate at 15 psi). This isn't specific to Instant Pot, however; it's true of all electric pressure cookers. Many pressure cooker recipes are written assuming the higher 15 psi pressure, so a few minutes of additional cook time may need to be added when using the Instant Pot.

Anyone who wants to own a slow cooker, pressure cooker, and rice cooker, but doesn't have the space to store all three, and who values quick, convenient cooking, and the "set it and forget it" aspect of slow cookers would love Instant Pot. Instant Pot comes with an instruction manual and short booklet of recipes. While basic and brief, the instruction manual covers all of Instant Pot's functions, as well as the recommended ratio of ingredients (like grains and dried beans) to water, and the cook times for popular items.

Reasons Why You Need An Instant Pot

Cook Beans Super Fast:
This is the first thing that piqued my interest. I heard that people were cooking beans in as little as 10-15 minutes for soaked beans and as long as 35-40 minutes for dry beans. Since it normally took several hours to slow cook beans this got my attention. I was really concerned that this was another single use appliance so I wasn't won over yet. Then I heard it again and again. People I really admire were in love with their Instant Pot and it officially landed on my wish list.

1. **Make Perfect Brown Rice:**

I've always thought that rice was really easy to cook. I know some people really struggle with it but it was easy for me. The first time I made brown rice in the Instant Pot I read and re-read the grain to water ratio. I was puzzled because it used less water and I was worried I would get crunchy rice. Guess what, it wasn't crunchy it was perfect! Perhaps the most perfect rice I've ever made with just the right amount of "stickiness."

Previously when I would have a busy day I'd cook rice in my Crock Pot. We love the Mexican Casserole and Cheezy Broccoli and Rice Casserole but some readers found it too mushy. The Instant Pot made these recipes perfectly in a fraction of the time. No more mushy rice.

2. **Steam/Cook Veggies in Minutes:**

When I hold local classes I usually admit that my method of cooking is to start cooking, walk away and forget I'm cooking, smell the food later then go back to the stove to check on it. That is why all of my recipes are so simple and easy. I've burned more than my fair share of veggies by forgetting about them. The Instant Pot cooks veggies in minutes. Just be sure to release the steam once they are finished cooking.

3. **Built in Timer:**

My favorite thing about Crock Pots is that you can leave and come back to fully cooked meals. My Instant Pot goes one step further. It has a timer so it won't start cooking until I want it to. Dinner doesn't have to start cooking in the morning and cook all day. You can program it to begin dinner at 4:30 and keep it warm until you get home.

Even if you are home during the day think about how much time you will save by setting it up during a spare moment and not thinking about it again until dinner time.

4. **Easy Clean Up:**

My least favorite thing to do in the kitchen is washing dishes. If I could outsource it, I totally would. Sometimes I don't cook a specific meal because I don't want to do the dishes. The Instant Pot is really easy to clean up. It comes with a big stainless steel pot and a lid. That is all you have to wash and it's really easy.

5. **Pressure Cooking Retains More Nutrients:**

This one I'll have to leave to the experts but I've read that pressure cooking retains more nutrients because foods cook for a shorter amount of time and less water is used. Due to the high pressure, beans and grains become more digestible. So, if you've avoided beans and grains due to stomach issues this MAY help. (I'm not a doctor or scientist so don't eat something that could make you sick.)

6. **They are Safe:**

You and I have all heard crazy stories of pressure cookers blowing up. I've resisted pressure cookers in the past because they scared me. The Instant Pot is safe! There are 10 safety features built-in to the Instant Pot including automatic pressure control, high temperature warning, and a lid that locks while pressurized plus many more.

7. **Slow Cooker:**

The Instant Pot is roughly the same size as my slow cooker (it's a little taller) but it does the same job with the touch of a button. If you plan to use your Instant Pot as a slow cooker regularly be sure to purchase the optional lid.

8. **Sauté Feature:**

The Instant Pot can also sauté with the touch of a button. So you can toss onions and garlic in, select sauté, get the rest of your ingredients ready and then add them to the pot and program it to make Soup or whatever else your heart desires.

Functions/Keys Of An Instant Pot

1. **Manual / Pressure Buttons:**

This is probably going to be the buttons you use most on the Instant Pot. It will allow you to pressure cook and manually select the time you want – rather than the preset buttons (such as Soup/Stew or Meat buttons). You can adjust the pressure, temperature and time by selecting the "+/-" buttons. Be sure to follow recipes (and add at least 1/2 cup to 1 cup of liquid to the inner pot) and note whether meals should be cooked at low or high pressure. The Instant Pot does default to High Pressure when the "Manual" button is selected, so adjust accordingly. And remember that the "Manual" / "Pressure" buttons are for pressure cooking – not for other functions like sauté, yogurt making or slow cooker (which don't require pressure cooking)

High Pressure
10.2 to 11.6 psi
239°F to 244°F
Low Pressure
5.8 to 7.2 psi
229 to 233°F

Note: The newer models of the Instant Pot have the same feature – it's called the "Pressure Cook" button.

2. **Sauté Button:**

The "Sauté" Button is the second most used function with my Instant Pot. You can do that and basically cook up anything as you would in a skillet or pan. You don't need the 1 cup of liquid. Just press the "Sauté" button, add some cooking oil (l like avocado or coconut) or animal fat like beef tallow or lard to the inner pot and add food you want to cook like a skillet or pan.

You can even adjust the sauté temperature:
Normal mode: 320 to 349°F
More mode: 347 to 410°F
Less mode: 275 to 302°F

I often start with the "Sauté" function and then use the "Manual" / "Pressure" button to then pressure cook my meal. It's fantastic to be able to use one pot for easy clean-up.

3. **Slow Cook Button:**

Use your Instant Pot like a slower cooker with this option. Just add food as you normally would to a slow cooker, close the lid (or use a slow cooker lid) and then press the "Slow Cook" button.

It will default to a 4-hour slow cook time. You can use "+/-" buttons to adjust the cook time.

4. **Bean / Chili:**

One of my favorite things to make in the Instant Pot is beans. It's so much faster (and tastier) with the Instant Pot. When you use the "Bean / Chili" button, it will default to a High Pressure for 30 minutes. You can adjust for "More" to High Pressure for 40 minutes or "Less" for High Pressure for 25 minutes. Typically, black beans take about 10-15 minutes, while kidney beans take 20-25. Refer to the Instant Pot Manual for cooking times for various beans and legumes. My Homemade Chili normally takes about 2-3 hours in the slow cooker, but with the Instant Pot it's just 25 minutes. I use a Natural Release for 5-10 minutes.

5. **Meat / Stew:**

Make your favorite stew or meat dish in the Instant Pot. Adjust the settings depending on the texture you want. For instance, the "More" setting is better for fall-off-the-bone cooking. It will default to a High Pressure for 35 minutes. You can adjust for "More" to High Pressure for 45 minutes or "Less" for High Pressure for 20 minutes. For a homemade stew with about 1-2 lb. of meat, I typically set to "Meat / Stew" in the Normal setting (high pressure for 35 minutes) and Natural Release for 10 minutes.

6. **Multigrain:**

The "Multigrain" button is best for cooking brown rice and wild rice, which typically takes longer than white rice to cook. Cook brown rice to a 1:1.25 ratio rice to water and wild rice to a 1:3 ratio rice to water for 22-30 minutes.
It will default at the "Normal" setting is 40 minutes of pressure cooking time. Adjust as needed for the "Less" setting is 20 minutes of pressure cooking time, or "More" at 45 minutes of warm water soaking and 60 minutes of pressure cooking.

7. **Porridge:**

Use the "Porridge" button to make rice porridge (congee) and other grains (not regular white or brown rice). It will default to a High Pressure for 20 minutes, which is best for rice porridge. You can adjust for "More" to High Pressure for 30 minutes or "Less" for High Pressure for 15 minutes. After the porridge is finished, do not use the QR handle. Because it has a high starch content, using the QR will splatter the porridge through the steam release vent. Use the Natural Rrelease.

8. **Poultry:**

Make your favorite chicken recipes with the "Poultry" button with the Instant Pot. It will default to a High Pressure for 15 minutes. You can adjust for "More" to High Pressure for 30 minutes or "Less" for High Pressure for 5 minutes.
I love to make shredded chicken for homemade tacos and burrito bowls. Add about 1 lb. uncooked chicken, 1/2 onion, 1 clove garlic minced, 1 cup bone broth, 1 tsp cumin, 1/2 tsp oregano, 1/8 tsp paprika, and 1/4 cup homemade salsa. Place lid on and set to "Poultry" to the default at High Pressure for 15 minutes. NR for 10 minutes and then QR. Open lid, use a fork and tongs to shred chicken and add salt and pepper to taste.

9. **Rice:**

You can cook rice in the Instant Pot in nearly half the time as a conventional rice cooker. White rice, short grain, Jasmine and Basmati rice can all be cooked on this setting in about 4 to 8 minutes. In general, you'll need a 1:1 ratio of rice to water (Basmati is a 1:1.5 ratio). When you choose the "Rice" button, the cooking duration automatically adjusts depending on how much food you put into the unit and cook on low pressure. Be sure to add about 10-12 minutes to the total cooking time to allow the Instant Pot to come to pressure.

Personally, I prefer to cook rice in the "Manual" mode at high pressure. I add 1:1 ratio of rice to water to the Instant Pot and set to 3 minutes with a 12 minutes Natural Release.

10. **Soup:**

Use the "Soup" button to make broth, stock or soup. The Instant Pot will control the pressure and temperature so that the liquid doesn't heavily boil. You can adjust the cooking time as needed, typically between 20-40 minutes, and the pressure to either low or high. Make a homemade bone broth WAY faster than the conventional slow cooker. Select the "Soup" button, set the pressure to low, and set the cooking time to 120 minutes. Once it's done, let the bone broth Natural Release for about an hour.

11. **Steam:**

Use the "Steam" button to steam vegetables, seafood or reheat food (it's a great alternative to the microwave). Be sure to use the steam rack included with the Instant Pot, otherwise food may burn and stick to the bottom of the inner pot.

Add 1-2 cups of water to the inner pot, place the steam rack inside the inner pot and with a stainless steel steam basket on top. Add vegetables, seafood, etc. in the basket. Press the "Steam" button and then adjust the time using the "+" or "-" key. Foods like frozen corn on the cob or a fresh fish filet will take 3-5 minutes, while fresh artichokes could take 9-11 minutes. Refer to the Instant Pot Manual for cooking times for various foods. Make homemade yogurt in the Instant Pot with glass bottles (such as Mason jars).

It's basically a 2-step process:
- Add milk to glass containers. Add 1 cup water to the inner pot, put in steam wrap and place glass containers filled with milk on top of the steam rack. Select the "Steam" function and set the time for 1 minute. Use NR. Keep the water in the inner pot.
- Let the milk cool below 115°F and then add yogurt starter or yogurt from another batch (or store-bought). Press the "Yogurt" button and adjust to "Normal" mode and adjust time based on your recipe. When the yogurt is done, it will display "yogurt".

12. **Keep Warm / Cancel Button:**

Once the Instant Pot is done cooking, you can use the "Keep Warm" / "Cancel" function to keep food hot or to cancel the pressure cooking mode.

- **Keep Warm Button:**

When pressure cooking is done, the Instant Pot will beep and automatically go into the "Keep Warm" function. It will display an "L" in front of a number to indicate how long it's been warm – e.g. "L0:30" for 30 minutes. It's a great feature to keep food warm (145 to 172°F) for up to 99 hours, 50 minutes. It's perfect for pot lucks.

- **Cancel Button:**

At any time, you can cancel cooking and return to standby mode by pressing the "Keep Warm" / "Cancel" button. This is a great option if you selected the wrong time for pressure cooking and need to stop to make adjustments to the pressure or time.

13. **Timer Button:**

Use the Timer button to delay the cooking start time for the Instant Pot. This works for both pressure cooking and slow cook options.

To use this feature, just press the Timer button with 10 seconds of pressing either the Pressure / Manual button or Slow Cook button. Use "+/-" buttons to adjust the delayed hours, then wait a second and press Timer again to set delayed minutes. You can cancel the Timer anytime by pressing the Keep Warm / Cancel button.

How to Clean Your Instant Pot Effectively

Step 1: Unplug

First things first, make sure your Instant Pot is unplugged before you start cleaning. It's a good idea to unplug your Instant Pot whenever it's not in use, but on this occasion in particular, you'll want to make sure it's unplugged for the intensive cleaning you're about to do, both for your safety and also for the safety of your appliance.

Step 2: Cleaning housing unit

While the outside housing unit definitely can't go in the dishwasher, you should be able to clean it thoroughly with a rag. Get the rag good and damp with water and cleaning solution, and wipe down both the inside and outside of the main housing unit (the exterior of the appliance, which holds the inner pot). For an even more thorough cleaning, use a sponge to get those hard-to-remove food bits and mineral deposits. Don't forget the nooks and crannies where little particles like to lodge!

Step 3: Wash lid

Next, you'll want to give the lid a good wash. You can hand-wash it in the sink with warm water, and be sure to add a little dish soap to make sure you're removing any and all bacteria and other nasty things you definitely don't want in your food. You might need to use a vinegar solution to get rid of all residual smells.

Step 4: Check other crevices

The Instant Pot has some nooks and crannies that you might not think to clean all the time. Now is the time to get all those crevices and small parts where food residue may build up over time. Remove the Quick Release handle, and wash it with warm, soapy water. Check around the steam valve, which can get blocked if too much deposit builds up there. Remove the shield, located inside the lid, which blocks the valve. Depending on the model you own, the shield could pop off easily, or it may need to be unscrewed. Check your owner's manual, or play around with it unless you've removed it. Wash the shield in the sink. Lastly, take a look at the condensation collection cup, which should be located on the side of your appliance. It may have collected food residue over time, so give it a scrubbing in the sink if it looks like it needs a cleaning.

Step 5: clean sealing ring

The silicone ring that can be found on the underside of the lid will likely need a thorough cleaning. After all, that's what ensures your Instant Pot has a tight seal, and it's an easy spot for food particles or residual smells to lurk. You should also check it for any signs of damage, as silicone can start to crack over time. If you notice any tears in the silicone ring, you'll want to order a replacement immediately. The silicone ring is dishwasher-safe, so you can pop it in there on the top rack. Once it's thoroughly cleaned, place it back on the underside of the lid, and make sure you've got a secure fit.

Step 6: Wash the inner pot

The inner pot is dishwasher-safe, so you should be washing this regularly anyway. But since you're doing a deep clean, it doesn't hurt to pop the inner pot into the dishwasher, along with any of the other dishwasher-safe accessories you use with your Instant Pot, such as silicone molds and wire racks. Once the inner pot is out of the dishwasher, dry it off with a paper towel and use some household vinegar to give it a thorough wipe-down. This gets rid of any built-up residue from things like minerals in your water, or dish detergent. After all, you want your Instant Pot to look nice and shiny, don't you? This will help with any smells as well.

Step 7: Steam clean and let dry

Now that everything is clean, you can reassemble everything. Don't forget about those small, easy-to-miss pieces, like the sealing ring and shield. Those are extra important to ensure you're using your Instant Pot safely, so definitely don't forget about them. Just in case the sealing ring still has a strange food smell, you can go a step further and deodorize the part with a vinegar steam clean. It's a simple process and can be done directly in the Instant Pot. Just add one cup of water, one cup of vinegar, and some lemon peels (for extra freshness!) to the inner pot, and run the Instant Pot's "Steam" setting for a few minutes. Be sure to allow pressure to release naturally, and when the lid is safe to open, you can remove the sealing ring and let it dry on the kitchen counter.

Instant Pot Must-Have Tools

1. **Sealing ring:**

There is a silicone ring inside of the lid. This ring can last for about 6 to 18 months. You have to separate the sealing rings for sweet and savory foods because the ring can retain strong odors.

2. **Glass lid:**

The pressure cooker has tempered glass lids that are good for slow-cooker setting so you can see the food in the pot.

3. **Round cake pans and casserole dishes:**

The pressure cooker has a 7inch round spring form pan for cheesecake, 7-inch cake pans, and 1½ quart soufflé or ramekins that will fit inside the pressure cooking pot. The large capacity Instant Pots can hold larger sizes. It is important to always measure and check to see if the pan or dish fits.

4. **Mini silicone oven mitts:**

The pressure cooker has a mini silicone oven. You can use any oven mitts, but I will recommend the miniature ones because they handy for safely gripping the lid of the very hot inner pot.

5. **Steaming baskets:**

Expandable metal steamer baskets, silicone or wire mesh can be used. The steamer basket can be used to keep hard-boiled eggs or steam veggies foods off the bottom of the Instant Pot. You can use the steamer basket when making broth and keep your bones in the basket for easy straining afterward.

BREAKFAST RECIPES

Breakfast Casserole

Preparation Time: 10 minutes

Cooking Time: 15 minutes

Total Time: 25 minutes

Serves: 5

Smart Points: 6

Ingredients:

- 1 1/2 cups of quinoa, soaked in water for about an hour
- 1 1/2 cups of water
- 1 tsp. ground cinnamon
- 1/4 tsp. salt
- 1 (15 oz.) can coconut milk, or any available milk
- 2 tsp. vanilla extract
- 1/4 cup pure maple syrup

Optional Ingredients include: Hemp hearts, Fresh fruit, Non-diary milk or Coconut flakes

Cooking Instructions:

1. After soaking the quinoa for an hour, drain and rinse well. Take your cinnamon, water, coconut milk, maple syrup, salt and vanilla.

2. Mix it along with quinoa in the bowl of your Instant Pot. Carefully keep the lid sealed and press the button to cook on low pressure for about 13 minutes.

3. Do not open the vent at the top or remove the lid until you allow the pressure to be release by itself for about 12 minutes.

4. Take 5 different bowls and put 1 cup of the quinoa with lids in each of the containers and store them in the fridge

5. Serve with the optional ingredients like Hemp hearts, Fresh fruit, Non-diary milk or Coconut flakes.

Egg Muffins

Preparation time: 10 minutes

Cooking time: 15 minutes

Total time: 25 minutes

Servings: 5

Ingredients:

- Cooking spray (Non spray)
- 7 large eggs
- ¼ tsp. salt
- 2 sliced scallions white and green parts
- ¼ cup 55ml milk
- 1/3 cup 28g shredded Parmesan cheese
- 1 cup (30 g) fresh baby spinach, chopped
- ½ cup (90 g) diced seeded tomato
- 2 sliced scallions white and green parts

Cooking Instructions:

1. Using a nonstick cooking spray, Spray 8 (160g) ovenproof custard cups. Whisk the eggs, milk, salt, and pepper until well blended as desired using a large bowl.

2. Take the custard cups and divide the spinach, tomato, and scallions equally. Take the egg mixture and pure over the veggies and Sporadically Sprinkle the Parmesan.

3. Place a trivet in the bottom of the pressure cooking pot Place and pour 1 cup of water (225ml). Take 4 out of the 8 custard cups.

4. Keep them on the trivet and also take another trivet and keep on top. Take also the remaining 4 custard cups and keep on it.

5. Do not forget to close the lid. Manually press the High Pressure button and cook it for about 5 minutes. When the timer beeps, do a natural pressure release for 6 minutes.

6. When the cook time ends, turn off the pressure cooker. Let the pressure release naturally for 5 minutes and finish with a quick pressure release

7. Open the lid and remove the cup when you observe the valve drops. Serve and enjoy the delicacy.

Creamy Taste Pumpkin Maple Oat

Preparation time: 7 minutes

Cooking time: 15 minutes

Total time: 22 minutes

Servings: 6

Ingredients:

- 1 cup steel cut oats (gluten-free)
- 1 1/3 cups water
- 1/2 teaspoon salt
- 1 tsp vanilla
- 1/3 cup pumpkin
- 4 tsp maple syrup
- 1/3 teaspoon cinnamon
- 1 13oz can coconut milk
- 1 tsp coconut sugar

Cooking Instructions:

1. Add the oats, coconut milk, water, salt and vanilla into a 4-quart instant pot.

2. Close and lock the lid. Manually set the timer for about 12 minutes and start cooking.

3. At the end of the 12 minutes, give another 10 minutes for the oatmeal to release natural thereafter, release the pressure.

4. Add maple syrup, coconut sugar, cinnamon and pumpkin.

5. Your creamy taste pumpkin maple oat is ready.

6. Serve and enjoy.

Pumpkin Apple Butter

Preparation time: 7 minutes

Cooking time: 13 minutes

Total time: 20 minutes

Yield: 5-6 Cups

Servings: 4

Ingredients:

- 1 tbsp spice of pumpkin pie
- 2 cans pumpkin puree (17oz each)
- Fingertip of salt
- 5 apples, peeled and sliced into tiny pieces
- 1 bottle of hard apple cider (14oz)
- 1 cup white sugar
- 1/4 cup honey

Cooking Instructions:

1. Add all the ingredients in a medium bowl and give everything a good mix. Add the ingredients into the bottom of your Instant Pot.

2. Set your pressure cooker to high pressure, gather all your ingredients, mix until it blends, and cook for about 13 minutes.

3. Carry out a natural release for at least 20 minutes and do a quick release for any pressure that remains.

4. Take out your butter and allow it cool completely then get some containers and put the butter according to your desired quantity and put them in your refrigerator.

5. Serve and enjoy.

Hard-Boiled Eggs

Preparation time: 6 minutes

Cooking time: 7 minutes

Total Time: 13 minutes

Servings: 5

Ingredients:

- Instant Pot rack
- 5 large eggs
- 1 cup water

Cooking Instructions:

1. Put the eggs on the rack and pour water in the pot while you keep the rack at the bottom of the pot.

2. Manually set the cooker on high pressure and cook for 7 minutes.

3. Let the pressure release naturally for about 7 minutes.

4. Remove the eggs and put in cold water and peel it when it is cool.

5. Serve and enjoy.

Pepper Frittata And Broccoli Ham

Preparation Time: 15 minutes

Cooking Time: 40 minutes

Total Time: 55 minutes

Servings: 6

Calories: 435 kcal

Ingredients:

- 2 cups of frozen broccoli
- 6oz ham cubed
- 1 cup sliced sweet peppers
- 2 tsp. ground pepper
- 6 eggs
- 1 cup sliced cheddar cheese
- 1 tsp. salt
- 1 cup half and half

Cooking Instructions:

1. Get a 6 x 3 pan and used a silicone brush to get oil or butter all over the pan. This is to avoid scraping out egg because you forgot to grease a corner.

2. Arrange the sliced sweet peppers in the bottom of the pan and Place the cubed ham on top of it and cover with frozen broccoli.

3. In a mixing bowl whisk together the eggs, half and half, salt, and pepper. Stir In shredded cheese.

4. Pour the egg mixture on top of your vegetables and ham and cover with foil or a silicone lid. In the inner liner of your Instant Pot and add 2 cups of water.

5. Place a steamer rack on top of this. Place the covered pan on the steamer rack. Set the cooker on high pressure and cook for about 25 minutes.

6. Allow it to release pressure naturally for 10 minutes before you release all remaining pressure. Gently use a knife to loosen the sides of what you have cooked.

7. Place a plate on top of the pan, and thump out the frittata onto the plate to your desired side facing up. Serve and enjoy.

Regular Oatmeal

Preparation time: 6 minutes

Cooking time: 7 minutes

Total Time: 13 minutes

Servings: 5

Ingredients:

- 1 cup of regular oats
- 3 cups of water or depending on your desired thickness of your Oatmeal.

Optional Toppings: apples, blueberries, strawberries, bananas, pears, sliced dates, cinnamon, flax seed, flax seed, maple syrup or agave, all kinds of nuts, coconut flakes, or peanut butter etc.

Cooking Instructions:

1. Take your Instant Pot, put water and regular oats. Cover the lid on the Instant Pot and press the manual button setting it to about 7 minutes.

2. Set the cooker on high pressure and cook for about 7 minutes. Allow it to release pressure naturally for 10 minutes before you release all remaining pressure.

3. Remove the lid. Put the oatmeal to a bowl, and put optional toppings.

4. Serve and store remains in a container in the fridge for about 7 days.

Breakfast Quinoa

Preparation Time: 20 minutes

Cooking Time: 5 minutes

Total time: 25 minutes

Servings: 5

Ingredients:

- 2 cups of well rinsed uncooked quinoa
- 1/2 tsp. vanilla
- 3 cups of water
- fingertip of salt
- 2 tbsp. maple syrup
- 1/3 tsp. ground cinnamon

Optional Toppings: milk, fresh berries, sliced almonds

Cooking Instructions:

1. Mix quinoa with water, maple syrup, vanilla, cinnamon, and salt to the pressure cooking pot. Manually select high pressure and 5 minutes cook time.

2. When beep sounds turn pressure cooker off, wait 10 minutes, and then use a Quick Pressure Release to release any remaining pressure.

3. Carefully remove lid, turning away from you to allow steam to disperse.

4. Serve the hot quinoa with milk, berries, and sliced almonds.

Buckwheat Porridge

Preparation Time: 8 minutes

Cooking Time: 30 minutes

Total time: 38 minutes

Servings: 6

Ingredients:

- 1 cup raw buckwheat
- 3 cups rice milk
- 1 sliced banana
- 1/4 cup raisins
- 1 tsp. ground cinnamon
- 1/2 tsp. vanilla

Cooking Instructions:

1. Rinse buckwheat well and put in Instant Pot.

2. Put all the ingredients and close the lid and making sure the steam release is in the closed position;

3. Select Manual, High Pressure for 6 minutes. When timer beeps, turn pot off and allow time for the natural release of pressure for about 20 minutes.

4. Carefully open lid and stir porridge with a long-handled spoon.

5. Serve and enjoy.

Blueberry Breakfast

Preparation Time: 5 minutes

Cooking Time: 6 minutes

Total time: 11 minutes

Servings: 6

Ingredients:

- 1/3 cup old fashioned oats
- 1/4 cup unsweetened almond milk
- 1/3 cup fat free Greek yogurt
- 1/4 cup blueberries, fresh or frozen
- 1 tbsp. sweetener
- splash of vanilla
- 1 1/2 cups of water
- fingertip of salt
- splash of cinnamon
- 1 Tbsp. chia seeds

Cooking Instructions:

1. Add water in your Instant Pot. Add all ingredients in the order given.

2. Close top of jar with a piece of aluminum foil and place in the pot.

3. Select Manual, High Pressure for 6 minutes. Allow your pressure cooker to release pressure naturally.

4. Carefully take out jar using a pot holder and set it on the counter to cool for a few minutes.

5. Allow to cool. Serve and enjoy!

SOUP, STEW & CHILI RECIPES

Chicken Tortilla Soup

Preparation Time: 13 minutes

Cooking Time: 5 minutes

Total time: 28 minutes

Servings: 7

Ingredients:

- 1 cup black beans (saltless), drained and well rinsed
- 1 1/3 lb. raw chicken breasts (boneless skinless)
- 13 oz. chopped tomatoes with green chilies
- 15 oz. chopped tomatoes (saltless)
- 1 cup frozen corn dissolved
- 1 jalapeno chopped
- 2 cloves garlic finely chopped
- 1 tsp. ground cumin
- 1/3 tsp. black pepper
- 1 tsp. chili powder
- 1 medium onion chopped
- 1 tsp. Himalayan salt
- 5 cups of organic chicken stock, low sodium

Tortilla Strips:

- Olive oil cooking spray
- 6 organic corn tortillas
- Himalayan salt

Optional toppings - avocado, cheese, lime, Greek yogurt, cilantro

Cooking Instructions:

1. Put all the ingredients for the soup into your Instant Pot and stir to mix properly.
2. Manually set the cooker to 20 minutes. It will take about 10-15 minutes to come to pressure.
3. Carefully switch to quick release when the timer beeps. Use a hand towel to open the lid and make a cut on the chicken with two forks.
4. Serve and enjoy with optional toppings!

Beef Stew

Preparation Time: 13 minutes

Cooking Time: 50 minutes

Total time: 1 hour and 3 minutes

Servings: 7

Ingredients:

Stew Ingredients:

- 10 oz whole mushrooms
- 2 cups celery, cut into 1" pieces
- 1 big onion, halved, then chopped
- 1/2 cup tomato juice
- 1/2 tsp. salt
- 1/4 tsp. black pepper
- 2 lbs. beef chuck roast, trimmed and chopped into 1" cubes
- 3 cups carrots, peeled and chopped into 1" pieces

Thickening Ingredients:

- 2 cups of tomato puree
- 1 tbsp. corn starch

Cooking Instructions:

1. Gather all of the stew ingredients into the instant pot, cover the lid and set the cooker on manual for 40 minutes.

2. When the time is up, let the pressure naturally release for 10 minutes, then turn the pressure knob to quick release.

3. If in any case you release the pressure and when has not already been released, stir together the tomato puree and the cornstarch.

4. Add them to the pot, turn on the sauté function and cook until thickened. Check the seasoning.

5. Serve and enjoy.

Stuff Pepper Soup

Preparation Time: 13 minutes

Cooking Time: 10 minutes

Total time: 23 minutes

Servings: 7

Ingredients:

- 1 cup cooked brown or white rice
- 1 1/2 lbs. Extra Lean Ground Turkey
- 15 oz. can Tomato Sauce
- 2 cups chopped Green and Red Peppers
- 1 cup Onion, chopped
- 4 cups Beef Broth
- ½ teaspoon Basil
- 2 packets of Chili Seasoning
- 13 oz. can chopped Tomatoes with Roasted Garlic and Onions

Cooking Instructions:

1. Fry the meat and onion, put peppers, tomatoes and tomato sauce, broth, and spices. Select Manual, High Pressure for 8 minutes.

2. When the timer beeps, do a natural pressure release for 15 minutes.

3. Carefully open the lid.

4. Serve and enjoy

Turkey Chili

Preparation Time: 13 minutes

Cooking Time: 4 hour 10 minutes

Total time: 4 hours and 23 minutes

Servings: 5

Ingredients:

- 2 cups chicken broth
- 2 tbsp olive oil
- 1 Onion, chopped
- 2 15 oz cans diced tomatoes
- 3 cloves of garlic, minced
- 2 lbs. lean ground turkey
- 2 cups prepared Great Navy beans
- 1 4 oz can of green chili
- 1 1/2 tbsp. cumin
- 1 tbsp chili powder
- salt and pepper to taste
- 1 small butternut squash, peeled and chopped into tiny sizes

Optional Ingredients: cilantro and plain Greek yogurt all for garnish

Cooking Instructions:

1. Set Instant Pot to the Sauté feature. Put olive oil and onions and sauté for about 4 minutes.

2. Put garlic and stir until desired fragrance, about 30 seconds. Put ground turkey and brown until well cooked.

3. Put chicken broth, beans, tomatoes, squash, chili, cumin, chili powder, salt & pepper. Stir to mix well.

4. Close and turn the Instant Pot on to the Slow Cooker function. Cook on high pressure for 4 hours 10 minutes.

5. Serve with optional toppings.

Italian Wedding Soup

Preparation Time: 7 minutes

Cooking Time: 10 minutes

Total time: 17 minutes

Servings: 5

Ingredients:

- Parmesan Cheese
- Small Meatballs
- 5 cups of chicken stock
- 1 tsp of olive oil
- 1 ½ cup of spinach
- 1 cup of diced carrots
- 1/3 onion, chopped

Cooking Instructions:

1. Set Instant Pot to sauté feature and allow it heat up. Put 1 tsp. olive oil, onions and carrots and fry for sometimes.

2. Put chicken stock, meatballs. Select Manual, High Pressure for 10 minutes. When cooking time elapse, do a quick release.

3. Carefully open the lid and add in spinach. Stir until it fatigues.

4. Serve with Parmesan cheese.

Italian Sausage Stew

Preparation Time: 8 minutes

Cooking Time: 10 minutes

Total time: 18 minutes

Servings: 4

Ingredients:

- 1/3 tsp. cumin
- 2 tbsp. butter
- ½ tsp. marjoram
- ¼ lb. pastured ground pork
- ½ tsp. onion powder
- ½ tsp. garlic powder
- 1¼ tsp. basil
- Sea salt/pepper to taste
- ½ tsp. thyme
- 9 oz gluten free noodles
- ¼ tsp. cayenne
- 1 tsp. sea salt
- ¼ tsp. black pepper
- 1 medium onion, diced
- 3 carrots, diced
- 2 stalks of celery, diced
- 4 ½ cloves of garlic, finely chopped
- ½ cup white wine
- Freshly grated parm to garnish
- 17 oz. can organic minced tomatoes
- 2 quarts bone broth
- 3 big handfuls chopped kale

Cooking Instructions:

1. Keep the Instant Pot on sauté feature. Put butter, pork and all of the seasonings. Stir to combine and brown the meat.

2. Put the onion, carrot, celery, and garlic, mix and cook for 5-7 minutes until the meats are soft and sweet.

3. Put the white wine to detach the pan scraping up any bits at the bottom. Put the minced tomatoes, broth, kale and noodles and stir to mix properly.

4. Keep the Instant Pot lid on making sure the valve is completely sealed and pressure cook for 5 minutes.

5. Release the valve and season with salt and pepper to taste.

6. Serve with freshly grated parmesan and enjoy.

Beanless Beef Chili

Preparation Time: 8 minutes

Cooking Time: 25 minutes

Total time: 33 minutes

Servings: 5

Ingredients:

- 1 1/2 cups chopped carrots
- 2 cloves chopped garlic
- 1 tsp salt
- 1 big onion, diced
- 1/2 cup chopped celery
- 2 1/2 small cans of tomatoes with green chilies
- 1 cup of bell peppers, diced
- 1½ Lbs. ground beef
- 1 1/2 cups of zucchini, cut into half moons
- 2 tbsp. chili powder
- 1 tbsp. olive oil
- 1 tsp. ground cumin
- 1 tsp. oregano
- 1/4 tsp. cayenne pepper
- 14 oz. can tomato puree or tomato sauce

Cooking Instructions:

1. Set your Instant Pot to sauté feature and brown beef until it is well cooked. Put garlic for the last minute to drain excess fat. You can set this aside.

2. Open the Instant pot and put oil, onions, celery, carrots, peppers and fry until onions are fatigued.

3. Put zucchini, tomatoes, cooked beef, and sauce into the Instant Pot and stir. Close and lock the lid in place.

4. Select Manual, High Pressure for 25 minutes. After cook time, switch to venting for quick pressure release.

5. Add toppings of your choice like avocado or cilantro

6. Serve and enjoy.

Broccoli Cheese Soup

Preparation Time: 7 minutes

Cooking Time: 5 minutes

Total time: 12 minutes

Servings: 4

Ingredients:

- 2 tsp. butter
- 1 medium onion, chopped
- 1 1/3 cups sharp cheddar cheese
- 1 cup chopped carrots
- 4 cups broccoli, roughly chopped (about 1/2 lb.)
- 2 cups cauliflower, diced (about 6 oz.)
- 1/2 tsp. salt & pepper, to taste
- 2 cups broccoli, chopped into small pieces (1/4 lbs.)
- 5 cups low-sodium chicken broth (1 (32 oz.)

Cooking Instructions:

1. Set the Instant Pot to sauté function, put the butter in your pot to melt. Add the onions and carrots in the butter until they start to soften.

2. Put the roughly chopped broccoli. Note, you don't need to add the broccoli that you chopped into small pieces yet.

3. Put the cauliflower, 1/2 tsp salt and the broth. Keep the lid on and set on manual for 3 minutes, quick release when it's finished.

4. If you have a regular blender, blend in batches everything inside the pot. Add the finely chopped broccoli.

5. Using few minutes, put back on sauté feature and cook until the broccoli has softened. Stir in the cheese, and put pepper to your desired taste.

6. Serve your meal!

Loaded Potato And Cauliflower Soup

Preparation Time: 8 minutes

Cooking Time: 8 minutes

Total time: 16 minutes

Servings: 4

Ingredients:

- 5 cups low-sodium chicken broth
- 1 1/4 cups sliced leeks
- 3 cloves garlic, diced
- 3 sliced scallions
- 3 1/2 cups of Yukon gold potatoes, peeled and diced
- 4 1/2 cups chopped cauliflower florets
- 1/3 cup of coconut milk (optional)
- 1 tsp. olive oil and 1 tsp butter
- 1/4 tsp. fresh ground black pepper
- 1 package of all-natural, nitrite-free turkey bacon cooked and minced
- Shredded cheddar cheese

Cooking Instructions:

1. Set Instant Pot to sauté mode and spray with cooking oil spray. Fry diced bacon, and then remove from pot.

2. Put in olive oil and butter, fry the leeks and garlic. Put cauliflower, potatoes, salt and stock.

3. Select Manual, High Pressure for 10 minutes. When the timer beeps, do a quick pressure release.

4. Use an immersion blender to blend everything and put coconut milk, if desired, then top with cheese, bacon.

5. Serve and enjoy.

Sweet Potato Chili

Preparation Time: 8 minutes

Cooking Time: 12 minutes

Total time: 20 minutes

Calories 335 kcal

Servings: 4

Ingredients:

- 1 can black beans drained
- 1 cup celery stalks, chopped
- 1 peeled and chopped sweet potato
- 1 big onion chopped
- 1 cup bell pepper
- 1 tsp. cayenne peppers
- 1/2 cup crushed tomatoes
- 2 cups chicken stock
- 1 Lb. ground turkey
- 1 tsp. cumin
- 2 chipotle peppers in adobo sauce
- 1 tbsp. diced garlic

Cooking Instructions:

1. Using sauté function, fry ground turkey and remove the grease from the pot. Add the garlic and onions and cook.

2. Combine cumin and cayenne pepper and add chipotle peppers, black beans, crushed tomatoes, sweet potatoes, and chicken stock.

3. Stir properly until everything is mixed. Close the lid and set pressure valve to sealing. Using the manual setting, cook on high pressure for 15 minutes.

4. Release pressure using the quick release method when cooking time is up. Carefully open the lid and switch Instant Pot to sauté mode.

5. Put your bell peppers and celery. Allow for about 8 minutes until the celery is well cooked. Switch off Instant Pot and Top with cheese, cilantro, and avocado.

6. Serve and enjoy.

Red Wine Beef Stew

Total time: 1 hour 40 minutes

Calories 550 kcal

Servings: 5

Ingredients:

- 3 lbs. boneless beef chuck cut into small pieces
- 3 tbsp. olive oil
- 1 tsp. corn starch
- 1 1/2 cups pearl onions frozen, dissolved
- 1 Lb. carrots cut into 2-inch sections
- 4-inch rosemary sprig
- 5-inch thyme sprig
- 1 tsp. sale
- 1 tsp. black pepper
- 1 1/3 cups red wine a big red, like a Syrah
- 5 dried figs stemmed

Cooking Instructions:

1. Set the sauté feature of the pressure cooker and heat the oil. Put the boneless beef, turn continuously for about 5 minutes and turn it to a big container.

2. Put onions and cook about 7 minutes. Put wine and stir, remove any browned bits on the bottom of the pan. Put carrots, figs, rosemary, thyme, salt and pepper.

3. Put the beef back to the pan. Close the lid on the pot and set the time for 35 minutes on high pressure.

4. Allow the pressure to reduce naturally for 25 minutes. When timer is done and carry out a quick pressure release.

5. Open the lid and remove the thyme and rosemary. Using a small container, whisk the cornstarch with 2 tsp water and Stir this into the pot, until thickened.

6. Optionally top rice, noodles, steamed potatoes.

7. Serve this wonderful dish.

Lemon Chicken Noodle Soup

Preparation Time: 10 minutes

Cooking Time: 25 minutes

Total time: 35 minutes

Ingredients:

- 1 cup chopped fresh flat-leaf parsley
- 1 1/2 cup chopped celery
- 1 tsp. salt, divided pepper, to taste
- 2 cloves of garlic, diced
- 2 big chicken breasts, trimmed (about 1 1/2 lbs. total)
- 3 cups chopped carrots
- 4 cups of low-sodium chicken broth (38 oz)
- 3 cups dry whole wheat egg noodles
- 2 lemons, zested and juiced (about 1/4 cup of lemon juice)
- 1 tsp. dried thyme
- 1 tsp. herbes d' provence
- 1 bundle green onions, whites and greens separated and chopped (about 1 cup, chopped)

Cooking Instructions:

1. Put olive oil or coconut oil into your Instant Pot. Switch on the saute function and fry the whites of the onions, celery and carrots.

2. Add the season with salt and pepper to taste, until the carrots start to brown a bit. Add the diced garlic and cook for sometimes.

3. Put the broth, chicken breasts to the pot, making sure that your chicken is completely covered by the broth.

4. Put the lid on your instant pot and turn the knob to "sealing" then set on manual for 10 minutes.

5. Press the "off" button when cooking time elapses, then do a quick pressure release by moving the knob on your lid from "sealing" to "venting position.

6. Carefully open the lid and remove the chicken to rest for a minute and keep them on a cutting board.

7. Put the dry pasta to the pot, put the lid back on setting it to "sealing" and set on manual for 0 minutes. While the pasta is cooking, cut the chicken with two forks.

8. Switch off your pot when the pasta is done, and again do a quick release, take off the lid and add the cut chicken back.

9. Put the lemon zest, lemon juice, thyme, herbes d' provence, parsley, the remaining green onions.

10. Serve and enjoy!

Chipotle Pumpkin Turkey Chili

Preparation Time: 8 minutes

Cooking Time: 15 minutes

Total time: 23 minutes

Servings: 4

Ingredients:

- 1 cup chicken broth (low-sodium)
- 1 1/2 red onion, chopped
- 1 big green bell chopped pepper
- 2 stalks of chopped celery
- 1 lb. lean ground turkey
- 1 tsp. cinnamon
- 2 1/2 tsp. cumin
- 1 Tbsp. chili powder
- 2 tsp. chipotle puree
- Salt
- 1 can (14 1/2 oz) petite diced tomatoes
- 1 can (15 oz) pumpkin puree
- 1 can well rinsed and drained (15 oz) black beans
- 2 cloves of garlic, diced

Optional Toppings: chopped cilantro and plain Greek yogurt

Cooking Instructions:

1. Set the Instant Pot to sauté mode, put the following on the pot - ground turkey and minced garlic salt and pepper.

2. Cook until the turkey turns brown. You may not completely cook the turkey because it'll later be cooked completely.

3. Put the peppers, onions and celery and cook one for sometimes while you sprinkle the cinnamon, cumin and chili powder.

4. Switch off the sauté mode, then put the tomatoes and the broth. Put the lid on your Instant Pot and set knob to "sealing".

5. Select Manual, High Pressure for 7 minutes. Turn the knob to "venting" for a quick pressure release when cooking time elapsed.

6. Switch on the sauté mode back, put the drained beans, the pumpkin puree and the chipotle puree and stir.

7. Put a bit more cinnamon, cumin and chili powder. Switch off the sauté mode and allow pressure release naturally and do quick release

8. Serve with the cilantro and plain Greek yogurt as your optional toppings.

BEANS, RICE & GRAIN RECIPES

Beans And Rice

Preparation Time: 8 minutes

Cooking Time: 45 minutes

Total time: 53 minutes

Servings: 5

Ingredients:

- Cooked rice
- 2 ls smoked sausage, sliced
- 2 clove garlic, chopped
- 2 Ls package Camellia Brand Red Kidney Beans
- 6 cups of water
- 1 tbsp oil
- 1 bay leaf
- Salt to taste
- Pepper to taste
- 1/4 stick of butter
- Cajun seasoning to taste
- 2 cups chopped seasoning blend from onions, celery, green bell peppers, parsley flakes

Cooking Instructions:

1. Sort beans and rinse well. Switch on the Sauté button on the Instant Pot. Put oil, add sliced sausage, and fry until browned.

2. When done, remove sausage and keep aside. Put 1/2 stick butter to your Instant Pot including the chopped seasoning blend and garlic.

3. Cook until onions turn soft and clear. Put cooked sausage back to pot, along with the beans, water, and bay leaf. Stir.

4. Switch Sauté mode off. Cover the lid and turn the valve to sealing. Press the Manual button and set to 30 minutes at high pressure.

5. When cooking time elapses, allow the pressure to release naturally for 25 minutes. Then, turn the valve to venting.

6. Open the lid, and use a spoon to mash beans to desired creamy consistency. Add salt, pepper, and Cajun seasoning to taste.

7. Serve with hot cooked rice and enjoy.

13 Bean Soup

Preparation Time: 6 minutes

Cooking Time: 15 minutes

Total time: 21 minutes

Servings: 4

Ingredients:

- 1 cup carrots, chopped
- 1 ham bone
- 1 big diced tomato
- 2 cups celery, minced
- 2 tsp. chili powder
- 1 tsp. garlic powder
- 1 tsp. sea salt
- 1 big diced tomato
- 1 big diced tomato
- 1/4 tsp. pepper
- 2 cups of 13 bean soup consisting of various beans, lentils, peas

Cooking Instructions:

1. Put your beans in the Instant Pot and put 3 $^{1/2}$ cups of water. Close and lock the lid in place. Select Manual, High Pressure for 15 minutes.

2. When the timer beeps, do a natural pressure release for about for 8-10 minutes. Carefully rinse and drain the beans.

3. Add the beans back into the Instant Pot and add the ham bone. Add enough water and cook, setting the cooker with a natural pressure release.

4. Take away the ham bone, add all the ingredients and cook on the soup setting for 15 minutes. Finally, release pressure naturally and do quick release.

5. Serve and enjoy!

Brown Rice And Beans

Preparation Time: 6 minutes

Cooking Time: 15 minutes

Total time: 21 minutes

Calories 270 kcal

Servings: 6

Ingredients:

- 2 1/2 cups short grain brown rice
- 1 onion chopped
- 2 red peppers diced
- 1 tbsp. taco seasoning
- 1 cup dried red beans
- 1 cup salsa
- 2 cups of vegetable or chicken stock
- 1 tsp. diced garlic
- 1/2 tbsp. avocado oil

Optional Toppings: cheese, sour cream, cilantro

Cooking Instructions:

1. Switch Instant Pot to sauté mode on high pressure and heat up. Put oil, onions, peppers, garlic and fry for at least 3 minutes.

2. Put rice, beans, salsa, seasonings and stock, stir thoroughly. Close and lock the lid in place. Switch off sauté mode.

3. Select Manual, High Pressure for 20 minutes. When the timer beeps, do a natural pressure release for about 10 minutes.

4. Serve with toppings of choice.

Baked Beans

Preparation Time: 7 minutes

Cooking Time: 40 minutes

Total time: 47 minutes

Servings: 6

Ingredients:

- 3 cloves garlic, diced
- 1 tsp. sea salt
- 2 Lb. small white beans
- 1 tbsp mustard powder
- 1 big onion, minced
- 1 cup molasses
- 1/2 cup maple syrup
- 1/4 tsp. ground pepper
- 5 cups of water
- 2 cups balsamic vinegar

Cooking Instructions:

1. Put the beans with 2 or 3 cups water into the Instant Pot and cook on high pressure for 10 minutes.

2. Rinse and drain the water out then place them back into the Instant Pot.

3. Put enough water and put all the ingredients.

4. Cook on bean setting for 40 minutes and release natural pressure.

5. Serve and enjoy.

Santa Fe Beans And Rice

Preparation Time: 10 minutes

Cooking Time: 25 minutes

Total time: 35 minutes

Servings: 5

Ingredients:

For the beans and rice:

- 1 (20 oz) can corn, rinsed and drained
- 2 cups long grain brown rice
- 2 cups water
- 1 (20 oz) can kidney beans, rinsed and drained
- 1 (10 oz) can tomato sauce
- 1 cup picante sauce
- 1 tsp salt
- 1/2 tsp pepper
- 1 (20 oz) can black beans, rinsed and drained
- 2 Tbsp taco seasoning

Optional Toppings: 1 1/2 lbs boneless, skinless chicken thighs or breasts

Grated cheddar

For the garlic lime sour cream:

- 2 tsp lime juice
- 1 tsp lime zest
- 1 cup sour cream
- 2 garlic cloves, diced
- 2 cups of chopped cilantro
- 1 tsp kosher salt

Cooking Instructions:

1. Put rice and water into the Instant pot. Without stirring, put the kidney beans, black beans, corn, tomato sauce, and picante sauce.

2. Add the taco seasoning, salt and pepper on top. Close the lid making sure valve is on sealing. Set Manual, High Pressure for 25 minutes.

3. When the timer beeps, do a natural pressure release for about for at least 7 minutes and remove the lid.

4. Prepare the garlic lime sour cream by mixing together sour cream, cilantro, lime zest, lime juice, kosher salt and garlic cloves.

5. Serve rice and beans with a dollop of the sour cream on top with a little topping of grated cheddar, if desired.

Pinto Beans

Preparation Time: 5 minutes

Cooking Time: 1 hour 25 minutes

Total time: 1 hour 30 minutes

Calories 180 kcal

Servings: 5

Ingredients:

- 5 cups of water
- 1 lb. dry pinto beans
- salt and pepper to taste
- 1 Tbsp Better Than Bullion vegetable base

Cooking Instructions:

1. Wash and drain your pinto beans using a wire mesh strainer.

2. Put them back into the Instant Pot with water and better than Bullion vegetable base.

3. Cover the lid, set to manual high pressure for 50 minutes and cook.

4. Release the pressure naturally and do quick release.

5. Serve and enjoy.

Refried Beans

Preparation Time: 5 minutes

Cooking Time: 30 minutes

Total time: 35 minutes

Servings: 5

Ingredients:

- 1 1/2 cup pinto beans, selected and washed
- 3 cups filtered water
- 1 medium onion
- 1 jalapeno, diced
- 1 tbsp sea salt
- ¼ cup avocado oil
- 1 bay leaf
- 2 cloves garlic, chopped

Cooking Instructions:

1. Put beans, water, bay leaf and garlic into the Instant Pot and cook on high pressure for 30 minutes and apply a natural release.

2. Turn the beans and water into a big container and set the Instant Pot to Fry mode.

3. Fry the onion and jalapeno in the olive oil and put the sea salt.

4. Put the beans and water back into the Instant Pot using the same settings.

5. Mix thoroughly the beans and cook until your refried beans are thickened.

6. Your dish is ready. Serve and enjoy!!!

Chicken Taco Bowl

Preparation Time: 5 minutes

Cooking Time: 30 minutes

Total time: 35 minutes

Calories: 270 kcal

Servings: 7

Ingredients:

- 2 cups long grain white rice, rinsed and drained
- 1 1/2 cups low sodium chicken broth
- 1 ½ packet taco seasoning
- 1 oz can black beans, rinsed and drained
- 2 chicken breasts
- 1 1/2 cups salsa
- 1 cup corn

Toppings: Sour cream, Cheese, Chopped cilantro, Chopped green onion, Sliced avocado

Cooking Instructions:

1. Spray the Instant Pot with non-stick cooking spray. Put 1/2 cup chicken broth into the bottom of your Instant Pot.

2. Put chicken breasts. Stir chicken with taco seasoning. Put black beans and corn. Add salsa.

3. Put rice and remaining 1 cup chicken broth. Put rice into the liquid, stir thoroughly and set valve to sealing. Cook on Manual for 8 minutes.

4. Allow pressure to naturally release for 10 minutes and do quick release. Slide rice to the side a bit to find the chicken breasts and pull them out.

5. Cut the chicken put a scoop of rice mixture to a bowl. Top with some chicken and other desired toppings.

6. Serve and enjoy.

Honey Garlic Chicken

Preparation Time: 5 minutes

Cooking Time: 30 minutes

Total time: 35 minutes

Calories: 340 kcal

Servings: 7

Ingredients:

- 1 tbsp sesame seed oil
- 1/3 cup honey
- 4 cloves garlic, minced
- salt and fresh ground pepper, to taste
- 1/2 cup no salt ketchup
- 1/2 tsp. dried oregano
- 2 tbsp. chopped fresh parsley
- 6 bone-in, skinless chicken thighs
- 1/2 tbsp. toasted sesame seeds, for garnish
- sliced green onions
- 1/2 cup low sodium soy sauce

Cooking Instructions:

1. Get a container and carefully mix honey, minced garlic, soy sauce, ketchup, oregano and parsley and set aside.

2. Set the Instant Pot to sauté mode and heat the pot. Add sesame oil to the pot. Put chicken thighs with salt and pepper and cook for about 3 minutes per side.

3. Put already prepared honey garlic sauce to the pot. Cover and close the lid. Cook in poultry mode for 20 minutes.

4. Turn off the pot and allow it to release the pressure, about 10 minutes. Put the chicken to a serving plate and scoop the sauce over the chicken.

5. You can garnish with toasted sesame seeds and green onions.

6. Serve and enjoy.

Butter Lemon Chicken

Preparation Time: 7 minutes

Cooking Time: 10 minutes

Total time: 17 minutes

Servings: 5

Ingredients:

- 2 pounds chicken breast or thighs
- 2 tbsp. ghee or butter
- 1 onion, diced
- 1 cup organic chicken broth
- 3 cloves diced garlic
- 1 tsp. salt
- 1 tsp. paprika
- ½ tsp. pepper
- 1 tsp. dried parsley
- ½ cup lemon juice, 2 lemons
- 3 tsp. arrowroot flour

Cooking Instructions:

1. Put the Instant Pot on sauté mode and add butter to melt. Put onion, garlic, paprika, parsley, and pepper and fry for about 2-3 minutes.

2. Using the same setting put the chicken and fry until it becomes brownish. Put chicken brother, lemon juice, and salt over chicken and stir.

3. Close lid and steam valve setting the Instant Pot to poultry mode and cook for 10 minutes. Release pressure naturally.

4. Remove the chicken from the Instant Pot, but leave the sauce in the pan.

5. Gently pour in arrowroot flour to thicken sauce.

6. Serve and enjoy.

Kung Pao Chicken

Preparation Time: 7 minutes

Cooking Time: 25 minutes

Total time: 32 minutes

Calories: 1805 kcal

Servings: 5

Ingredients:

For the chicken:

- Green onion to garnish
- 1 zucchini minced
- 1/2 red bell pepper diced
- 1/2 cup onion chopped red or white
- 3 1/2 garlic cloves diced
- 2 tbs vegetable oil
- 1 cup cashews or peanuts
- 1 1/2 lbs. Chicken skinless chicken breast

For the sauce:

- 1/4 tsp ground black pepper
- 2/3 cup garlic coconut aminos
- 1/2 tsp red pepper flakes
- 1/2 tsp ground ginger

Cooking Instructions:

1. Put oil to instant pot and fry chicken until it gets brownish. Put all vegetables and stir. Add the sauces.

2. Close and lock the lid. Select Manual, Low Pressure for 25 minutes. When the timer beeps, do a natural pressure release for about 10 minutes.

3. Carefully remove the lid.

4. Serve and enjoy!

Orange Chicken

Preparation Time: 7 minutes

Cooking Time: 20 minutes

Total time: 27 minutes

Servings: 5

Ingredients:

- 5 chicken breasts (not thin breasts).
- 3/4 cup favorite dark sweet barbecue sauce
- 2 tbs soy sauce
- 3/4 cup orange marmalade
- 2 tsp cornstarch
- chopped green onions for garnish

Cooking Instructions:

1. Carefully cut chicken breasts into small sizes. Put chopped chicken, barbecue sauce, and soy sauce into your Instant pot.

2. Cook on Manual, High Pressure for 5 minutes. When the timer beeps, do a quick pressure release. Take 1/3 cup of the barbecue chicken sauce out of instant pot.

3. Mix it with cornstarch in a small container. Put cornstarch broth mixture back into Instant Pot.

4. Put orange marmalade and stir properly. Set Instant Pot to sauté setting and fry for 8 minutes.

5. Keep it to rest 7 minutes to make the sauce thicker. Garnish with green onions.

6. Serve and enjoy with family!!!

Ground Turkey Lentil Chili

Preparation Time: 25 minutes

Cooking Time: 20 minutes

Total time: 45 minutes

Servings: 5

Ingredients:

- 1 (10 oz) can tomato sauce
- 2 lb. ground turkey
- 2 diced garlic cloves
- 2 Tbsp. tomato paste
- 1/2 tsp. pepper
- 1 1/2 tsp. salt
- 1 ½ cup dry green lentils
- 2 cups water
- 1 (12 oz.) can petite diced tomatoes
- 1 (4 oz.) can diced green chiles
- 2 tsp. chili powder
- 1 tsp. cumin
- 1 medium yellow onion, diced

Cooking Instructions:

1. Switch your Instant Pot on to "sauté." Fry the ground turkey to brown.

2. Put the minced onions, garlic, tomato paste and salt and cook until meat is browned and onions are softened.

3. Put the lentils, water, tomato sauce, diced tomatoes, green chiles, chili powder, cumin and pepper.

4. Close the Instant Pot. Switch it to "manual," set the timer to 15 minutes and set the valve is set to "sealing."

5. When cooking time elapse, let it rest for 15 minutes and then slowly release the pressure. Carefully open the lid and scoop the chili into plates.

6. Top with a dollop of sour cream and some diced green onions.

7. Serve this delicious meal.

Korean Chicken Meatball

Preparation Time: 5 minutes

Cooking Time: 20 minutes

Total time: 25 minutes

Servings: 5

Ingredients:

- 2 eggs
- 2 lbs. ground chicken
- 1 1/2 tsp. olive oil
- 2 garlic cloves, minced
- 1 tbsp. grated ginger (not packed)
- 1 tsp. red pepper flakes
- 1/2 tbsp. sesame oil
- 1/2 cup panko crumbs
- 1/2 cup Korean BBQ Sauce
- 1/3 tsp. salt

Cooking Instructions:

1. Mix all the ingredients together except for the panko crumbs, Korean BBQ sauce, and green onions.

2. Put the panko crumbs over the chicken, mix and let the panko soak into the chicken mixture for 7 minutes.

3. Make about 10 balls, put the olive oil to the bottom of the Instant Pot and then put the chicken to the Instant Pot.

4. Select the poultry option and make sure it's sealed. Prepare the Korean BBQ Sauce while the balls are cooking. When the timer goes off, vent the Instant Pot.

5. Serve and enjoy!!!

Chicken And Dumplings

Preparation Time: 5 minutes

Cooking Time: 8 minutes

Total time: 13 minutes

Servings: 4

Ingredients:

- 2 cups chicken broth
- 1 cup water
- 1 teaspoon olive oil
- 1-1/2 lbs. chicken breast cubed
- 1 tube 16oz refrigerated biscuits
- 1 cup chopped carrots
- 1 cup frozen peas
- 2 teaspoons oregano
- 1/2 - 1 teaspoon onion powder
- 1/2- 1 teaspoon basil
- 1-2 cloves minced garlic
- 1/2 teaspoon salt
- 1/2 teaspoon pepper

Cooking Instructions:

1. Slice each biscuit to about 1/4 thickness. Using a knife, cut into 1/2" strips. Put 1 1/2 tsp. olive oil into the instant pot.

2. Add also chicken, oregano, onion powder, basil, garlic, salt and pepper and mix to your desired coat. Set your Instant Pot to sauté mode and cook chicken.

3. Cover the Lid and stir at intervals until it becomes brownish. After cooking time elapsed, switch off instant pot.

4. Put 2 cups of chicken broth and 1 cup of water, carrots and peas to instant pot and stir properly until mixed and add biscuits.

5. Cover lid of instant pot and close the pressure knob setting instant pot to manual for 5 minutes. When the timer beeps, do a quick pressure release.

6. Serve and enjoy.

Honey Lemon Chicken

Preparation Time: 12 minutes

Cooking Time: 35 minutes

Total time: 47 minutes

Calories: 370 kcal

Servings: 4

Ingredients:

- 3 cloves garlic, peeled and diced
- 1 lb. bone-in, skin-on chicken thighs
- 1 1/2 tsp. lemon pepper seasoning
- zest of one lemon
- 3 tbsp. honey
- 2 1/2 tbsp. water
- 1 tbsp. soy sauce
- 1 tsp. corn starch
- 1/3 cup freshly squeezed lemon juice (about 1 lemon)
- 1/3 cup water
- 2 tbsp. canola oil
- Corn starch Slurry for thickening of the sauce

Cooking Instructions:

1. Cut off chicken thighs of excess fat and season with lemon pepper seasoning. Set the Instant Pot on sauté mode.

2. Put oil when the pot is hot and heat with the Instant Pot lid open. Keep chicken in a single layer with skin side down.

3. Cook for about 3 minutes and then turn to cook for another 3 minutes. Remove surplus oil from the Instant Pot and put garlic and cook, for about 20 to 30 seconds.

4. Using a small bowl, mix lemon juice, lemon zest, honey, water, and soy sauce. Stir properly until well mixed and pour over chicken.

5. You can now press keep warm/cancel button. Close and lock the lid, and set the floating valve on Sealing.

6. Press the Poultry button and set the cooking time to 15 minutes. Do a quick release by pressing Cancel button.

7. If you want to reduce the sauce, press the sauté button and cook, with the lid open, for about 4 minutes.

8. On the other hand, you can add corn starch slurry and cook using Sauté mode for about 1 to 2 minutes or until sauce is thickened.

9. Serve and enjoy.

Chicken Tortilla-Less Soup

Preparation Time: 7 minutes

Cooking Time: 25 minutes

Total time: 32 minutes

Servings: 7

Ingredients:

For Soup:

- 1 tsp. dried oregano
- 1 tsp. onion powder
- 2 boneless skinless chicken breasts (about 1 lb.)
- 2 cans ROTEL, any variety
- 2 tsp. adobe sauce
- 1 medium chopped onion
- 2 tsp. garlic powder
- 1 tsp. cumin
- 2 tsp. chili powder
- 1 tsp. smoked paprika
- 2 chipotle peppers in adobo sauce
- 1 1/2 tsp. salt
- 2 zucchinis, chopped or cut into 1/2" half moons
- 1 15 oz. can Whole30-compliant chicken broth
- 1 14- oz. can full-fat coconut milk or coconut cream, whisked until smooth

Garnishes: fresh avocado slices, red onions, sliced thin, fresh cilantro

Cooking Instructions:

1. Pour salt on the boneless skinless chicken breasts. Put the chicken breasts to the Instant Pot and add the remaining ingredients.

2. Add the spices and top with zucchini. Cover the lid on the Instant Pot. Cook at high pressure for 20 minutes.

3. Let the pressure to naturally release for 12 minutes, and then use the manual release. Remove the chicken breasts and put coconut milk.

4. Turn Instant Pot to Sauté mode and stir to mix well. Dice chicken and return to soup. You can top with any garnish of choice.

5. Serve and enjoy!!!

Green Chili Chicken Enchilada Soup

Preparation Time: 7 minutes

Cooking Time: 25 minutes

Total time: 32 minutes

Servings: 7

Ingredients:

- 1 cup thick and chunky salsa verde
- 1 Tbsp. cumin
- 2 1/2 chicken breast halves (frozen or fresh)
- 4 1/2 cups water
- 2 tsp. Better Than Bouillon Chicken Base
- 2 Tbsp. lime juice
- 1 10 oz can green chile enchilada sauce
- 1 5 oz can green chiles
- 1 1/2 tsp. chili powder
- Salt and pepper
- 1 tsp. garlic powder
- 1/2 cup long grain brown rice, uncooked
- 1 13 oz can seasoned white beans, drained
- 1 1/2 cups frozen sweet white corn
- 4 oz cream cheese
- 1 tsp onion powder

Optional toppings: tortilla chips, grated cheese, sour cream, jalapenos, and cilantro

Cooking Instructions:

1. Put chicken, water, bouillon, enchilada sauce, green chiles, salsa, cumin, chili powder, onion powder, garlic powder, rice and beans to the Instant Pot.

2. Stir to mix properly. Close the pot, cover the lid and set valve to "sealing." Using high pressure set the manual timer to 25 minutes.

3. When cooking time elapse, let the pressure release naturally for at least 15 minutes. Open the lid. Keep the chicken on a cutting board and cut.

4. Put it back into the pot. Sprinkle the corn and cream cheese, until the cream cheese is melted. Put the lime juice and stir. Add Salt and pepper to taste.

5. Scoop into bowls and add toppings of your choice. Serve and enjoy!!!

BEEF & PORK RECIPES

Beef Stroganoff

Preparation Time: 8 minutes

Cooking Time: 25 minutes

Total time: 33 minutes

Calories 321 kcal

Servings: 5

Ingredients:

- 1 tbsp. oil
- 1/2 cup diced onions
- 1/2-1 tsp. pepper
- 1 tbsp Worcestershire sauce
- 1 tsp. salt
- 1 lb. pork tips or beef stew meat
- 3/4 cup water
- 1 tbsp. garlic
- 1.5 cups chopped mushrooms

For Finishing:

- 1/4 cup sour cream
- 1/3 tsp. xanthum gum (sub with arrowroot starch, corn starch or other thickener)

Cooking Instructions:

1. Switch Instant Pot on Sauté on high and put the oil, add onions and garlic when the oil is hot and stir for a while.

2. Put all ingredients except sour cream and close up the pot. Set the cooker to 25 minutes on high pressure. When the timer beeps, let it release pressure naturally.

3. Open the pot and turn it on to Sauté and add sour cream and stir. Shake in the xanthum gum a little at a time, and keep stirring until the mix thickens.

4. Scoop into plates and top with cauliflower rice or low carb noodles.

5. Serve and enjoy the meal.

Pulled Pork

Preparation Time: 30 minutes

Cooking Time: 50 minutes

Total time: 1 hour 20 minutes

Calories: 421 kcal

Servings: 5

Ingredients:

- 2 chipotle peppers in adobo sauce, diced
- 5 lb. boneless pork loin or boneless pork shoulder/butt
- 1 tsp. kosher salt
- 1/2 tsp black pepper
- bbq sauce (your favorite)
- 14 oz Dr Pepper soda

Cooking Instructions:

1. Cut pork into 6 pieces and season with salt and pepper.

2. Put pork in instant pot insert and top with diced chipotle peppers and sprinkle Dr Pepper around the pork.

3. Cover the lid on Instant Pot and seal. Press Manual, High Pressure to cook for 50 minutes. When the timer beeps, do a natural pressure release for 15 minutes.

4. Then, quick release the remaining pressure. Remove pork and put in a big bowl. Cut using two forks and add bbq sauce to your tastes.

5. Serve and enjoy.

Mongolian Beef

Preparation Time: 15 minutes

Cooking Time: 35 minutes

Total time: 50 minutes

Servings: 5

Ingredients:

- 8 cloves garlic, diced
- 1 tbsp. cornstarch
- 1 1/2 tbsp. extra virgin olive oil
- 1/2 cup brown sugar
- 1/2 cup lite soy sauce
- 1 lb. flank steak, sliced across the grain
- 1 cup water
- 1 tsp. red pepper flakes
- 1 tbsp. fresh ginger, diced

Cornstarch Slurry:

- 2 tbsp. cornstarch
- 1/2 cup water

Garnish:

- 1/3 cup green onions, chopped
- 1 tsp. sesame seeds

Cooking Instructions:

1. Set the Instant Pot to Sauté mode. When it is hot, put sliced beef to a big bag that can be zipped and put 1 tbsp cornstarch and shake well to coat the beef properly.

2. Put the oil to the hot Instant Pot, once the oil is hot, add the beef and sauté for about 3 minutes and stir for sometimes.

3. Put the rest of the ingredients to the pot: minced garlic, ginger, lite soy sauce, brown sugar, water, red pepper flakes and stir properly until all the ingredients are mixed and coated in sauce.

4. Cover lid and pressure cook at High Pressure for 10 minutes. Switch off the heat. Release the remaining pressure about 10 minutes.

5. Open the lid. Make the cornstarch slurry, in a small bowl mix cornstarch with water until fully mixed. Set the Instant Pot on the Sauté mode.

6. Add the cornstarch to the pot, stir to mix well and cook for 4 minutes stirring periodically, until the sauce thickens. Switch off the Instant Pot.

7. Let the Mongolian Beef rest for 12 minutes so that the sauce will settle and thicken more. Garnish with fresh chopped green onions and sesame seeds.

8. Serve and enjoy!!!

Spicy Thai Beef Nachos

Preparation Time: 13 minutes

Cooking Time: 9 minutes

Total time: 21 minutes

Servings: 5

Ingredients:

- 1 cup Carrot, chopped
- 25 Scooped Corn Chips
- ½ cup Cilantro, minced
- 1 ½ cups Cheese, shredded
- ½ lb. Roast Beef, sliced or shredded
- 1 Shallot, minced
- ½ cup Jarred Peanut Sauce
- Wedges of Lime for Spritzing
- Jarred Sliced Jalapenos
- 6 leaves Mint, diced

Cooking Instructions:

1. Spread Scooped corn chips and remove any broken chips.

2. Using a small container, mix sliced roast beef, carrot, shallot, mint, and cilantro. Spoon into chip cups. You may alternatively prepare like traditional nachos.

3. Top with shredded cheese and broil until cheese has melted and begins to bubble.

4. Take out from oven and drizzle with jarred peanut sauce, spritz with lime and top with sliced jalapeno if desired.

5. Serve immediately and enjoy.

Boneless Pork Chops

Preparation Time: 6 minutes

Cooking Time: 9 minutes

Total time: 15 minutes

Servings: 5

Ingredients:

- 1 stick of margarine
- 7 boneless pork chops
- 1 package of ranch mix
- 1 1/2 cup of water
- 1 tbsp. of coconut oil

Cooking Instructions:

1. Put the pork chops in the Instant pot and add a tbsp of coconut oil. Switch on the sauté mode and fry to brown on both sides.

2. Put the margarine on top and stir in the ranch mix packet on top. Put water over the pork and put the lid on and set to sealing.

3. Set the manual button to 7 minutes. Allow it to naturally release pressure for 5 minutes and then do a quick release to remove the remaining pressure.

4. Serve immediately and enjoy.

Korean Beef And Brown Rice

Preparation Time: 10 minutes

Cooking Time: 15 minutes

Total time: 25 minutes

Servings: 5

Ingredients:

For the rice:

- 1 Tbsp. sesame oil
- 1 1/2 cups long grain brown rice
- 2 cups water
- 1/2 tsp. salt

For the beef:

- 1/3 cup low sodium soy sauce
- 1 tsp. garlic powder
- 1/4 tsp. ground red pepper
- 2 tsp. diced ginger
- 1/3 cup brown sugar
- Toasted sesame seeds, for garnish
- 1 lb. lean ground beef
- Sliced green onions, for garnish
- 1 Tbsp. tomato paste

Cooking Instructions:

1. Cover the bottom of the Instant Pot with non-stick cooking spray to help to stick rice and clean up. Put the rice, water, and salt in the bottom of the Instant Pot.

2. Using an oven safe dish that fits inside your Instant Pot, stir together the brown sugar, soy sauce, sesame oil, garlic powder, red pepper, minced ginger and tomato paste.

3. Put the ground beef and break the beef up with a spoon. Stir the beef with the sauce to coat. Keep the oven safe dish on top of the trivet as you lower the trivet.

4. Dish on top of the rice/water in the bottom of the Instant pot. Close the Instant Pot, set the valve on sealing. Select Manual, High Pressure for 25 minutes.

5. Immediately cooking time elapses allow the pressure release naturally for about 10-12 minutes and then release the remaining pressure.

6. Remove the trivet and dish out of the instant pot. If the bottom of the trivet is left with some rice kernels on it stir the beef and break it up with a spoon.

7. Using a plate, scoop a portion of rice and then top with the beef and a bit of the juices or you may top with green onions and sesame seeds as you desire.

8. Serve immediately and enjoy!!!

Pork Tenderloin Teriyaki

Preparation Time: 15 minutes

Cooking Time: 35 minutes

Total time: 50 minutes

Servings: 5

Ingredients:

- 2 1/2 green onions chopped
- 2 tbsp oil
- 2 1/2 cups teriyaki sauce
- toasted sesame seeds
- 2 pork tenderloins (cut in half length)
- salt and pepper to taste

Cooking Instructions:

1. Take a bowl and season the pork with salt and pepper. Switch on your Instant pot and set to sauté mode, and put the oil in the bottom.

2. Observe when the pan is hot, then put the meat making sure it browns both sides of them. Add the browned meat in the cooker and pour the teriyaki sauce on top.

3. Cover and seal the lid. Select Manual, High Pressure for 20 minutes. Release the pressure naturally, and then remove the lid and cut the meat.

4. Scoop jasmine rice and steamed broccoli and garnish with toasted sesame seeds and chopped green onions.

5. Serve and enjoy.

Beef Pot Roast

Preparation Time: 15 minutes

Cooking Time: 1 hour 45 minutes

Total time: 2 hours

Servings: 7

Ingredients:

- 2 1/2 tbsp. corn starch
- 1 big bag carrots, peeled and chopped
- 4 1/2 (1 oz) packets of McCormick Brown Gravy Mix
- 1 cup brewed coffee
- 10 oz red wine (cabernet)
- 1/2 cup reduced sodium soy sauce
- 3 tbsp. Worcestershire sauce
- 2 tsp. freshly cracked black pepper
- 3 lb. bottom round roast
- 6 big cloves garlic, diced
- 1 big sweet yellow onion, chopped
- 2 cups sliced portobello mushrooms
- 2 tbsp. oil

Cooking Instructions:

1. Whisk together McCormick Brown Gravy Mix and cornstarch in a big container. To avoid lumps, whisk in coffee gently.

2. Whisk in wine, soy sauce, Worcestershire sauce, garlic and black pepper. Keep them in one corner. Set instant pot to sauté mode.

3. Put oil to pot and quickly sear meat on all sides. Switch off sauté mode. Top meat with carrots, onion and mushrooms, gravy mix on top.

4. Close and lock the lid in place. Switch Instant Pot on to manual and set for 1 hour 45 minutes using high pressure. Do a natural release for 15 minutes.

5. Take out roast from instant pot, cut with forks, put gravy and vegetables to mix well. Scoop your dish into a plate, top with gravy and vegetables over mashed potatoes.

6. Serve and enjoy

Smothered Pork Chops

Preparation Time: 15 minutes

Cooking Time: 27 minutes

Total time: 42 minutes

Servings: 5

Ingredients:

- 1 tbsp butter
- 1 tbsp paprika
- 1 1/2 tsp onion powder
- ½ tsp xanthan gum
- 1 tsp black pepper
- 1 tsp salt
- ¼ teaspoon cayenne pepper
- 2 tbsp coconut oil
- ½ medium onion, sliced
- 5 oz sliced baby bella mushrooms
- ½ cup heavy cream
- 1 tbsp chopped fresh parsley
- 4 (6 oz) boneless pork loin chops
- 1 1/2 tsp garlic powder

Cooking Instructions:

1. Combine and mix these ingredients together in a small container - paprika, garlic powder, onion powder, black pepper, salt, and cayenne pepper

2. Wash the pork chops and pat dry. Spray both sides of the pork chops with 1 1/2 tbsp of the spice mixture, rubbing the seasoning into the meat. Do not use all the spices.

3. Set the Instant Pot on the Sauté mode put the coconut oil in the bowl of the pot. Fry the pork chops to brown for about 3 minutes per side.

4. Remove the pork chops from the Instant pot. Put the sliced onions and mushrooms into the pot. Add the browned pork chops.

5. Put the lid to Instant Pot and confirm the vent is sealed. Set the pot on the manual high pressure for 30 minutes.

6. When the cooking time elapses, the pressure can be released naturally. Open the pot lid and place just the pork chops on a serving plate.

7. Reset the Sauté mode again and whisk the remaining spice mixture, butter, and heavy cream into the hot liquid.

8. Pour 1/2 tsp of xanthan gum into the liquid and whisk in immediately. Let the gravy simmer for 5 minutes until the butter is melted and the sauce starts to thicken.

9. Switch off the Pot. Start with ¼ tsp of xanthan gum and put additional until the gravy thickens to your desired taste.

10. Sprinkle with parsley and serve and top the pork chops with the onion and mushroom gravy.

11. Serve and enjoy.

FISH & SEAFOOD RECIPES

Steamed Alaskan Crab Legs

Preparation Time: 6 minutes

Cooking Time: 5 minutes

Total time: 11 minutes

Servings: 5

Ingredients:

- 1 cup water
- 3 lbs. frozen crab legs
- Melted butter for serving
- 1/2 tbsp. salt

Cooking Instructions:

1. Take your Instant Pot Put steamer basket into Instant Pot with 1 cup of water and 1/2 tbsp of salt.

2. Put half of the Alaskan King Crab Legs with 1 tbsp of salt. Cover the lid of the Instant Pot and confirm the valve is set to sealing.

3. Manually adjust the time to 5 minutes on high pressure and allow the Instant pot to come to pressure.

4. Immediately cooking time finished switch the setting on top of your Instant Pot to release remaining pressure.

5. Open up your Instant Pot when the pin has dropped (this can take few minutes). Remove crab legs and top with melted butter.

6. Serve and enjoy.

Instant Pot Salmon

Preparation Time: 6 minutes

Cooking Time: 5 minutes

Total time: 11 minutes

Servings: 5

Ingredients:

- 5 fillets – salmon
- 2 medium lemon
- 1 tbsp. butter, unsalted
- 1/4 tsp. salt
- 1/4 tsp. black pepper, ground
- 3/4 cup water
- 1 bunch dill weed, fresh

Optional Toppings:

- 1 cup of brown rice, raw
- 4 cups of green beans

Cooking Instructions:

1. Put 1/4 cup fresh lemon juice, 3/4 cup of water in the bottom of the Instant Pot.

2. Put the metal steamer insert and put the salmon fillets, frozen, on top of the steamer insert.

3. Spray fresh dill on top of the salmon, and then keep one slice of fresh lemon on top of each one.

4. Close the Instant Pot lid then set the Manual timer for 5 minutes. Immediately cooking time finished, allow pressure to release naturally and do quick release.

5. Serve immediately and enjoy!!!

Shrimp Scampi

Preparation Time: 6 minutes

Cooking Time: 10 minutes

Total time: 16 minutes

Servings: 4

Ingredients:

- 1 tbsp. fresh squeezed lemon juice
- 2 tbsp. extra virgin olive oil
- 2 tbsp. pastured butter
- 1 tbsp. minced organic garlic
- 1/2 cup white wine
- 2 lbs. shrimp
- 1 lb. gluten free pasta or 3 cups cooked rice
- Sea salt and pepper, to taste
- Parsley, optional garnish
- 1/2 cup homemade chicken stock

Cooking Instructions:

1. Put the oil and butter in your Instant Pot, closing the lid and set the pot to Sauté mode. Heat the butter for a couple of minutes.

2. Add the garlic and cook just until fragrant. Put the white wine and chicken stock to deglaze the pot. Stir up any browned bits.

3. Switch off the Sauté mode, and put the shrimp and cover with the lid. Set to meat/stew for 1 minute.

4. When the timer beeps, do a natural pressure release for about 5 minutes, then use quick release to release the remaining pressure.

5. Sprinkle the cooked pasta or rice and add the lemon juice, salt and pepper to taste.

6. Serve immediately.

Lemon Pepper Salmon

Preparation Time: 6 minutes

Cooking Time: 10 minutes

Total time: 16 minutes

Servings: 4 - 5

Ingredients:

- 1 carrot chopped
- ¾ cup water
- 1 LB salmon filet skin on
- 1 zucchini chopped
- 3 tsp ghee
- ¼ tsp salt or to taste
- ½ tsp pepper or to taste
- 1/2 lemon thinly sliced
- 1 red bell pepper chopped
- A few sprigs of parsley dill, tarragon or a combo

Cooking Instructions:

1. Add water and herbs in the Instant Pot and then put in the steamer rack making sure the handles are properly extended.

2. Put salmon, skin down on rack and mix salmon with ghee/fat, season with salt and pepper, and cover with lemon slices.

3. Lock the Instant Pot and make sure vent is turned to "Sealing". Plug it in, press "Steam" and set it to 3 minutes.

4. Garnish your veggies while salmon is still being cooked. Immediately cooking time elapses, quick release the pressure. Press the "Warm/Cancel" button.

5. Open the lid, and using hot pads, carefully remove rack with salmon and set on a plate. Take away herbs and discard.

6. Put veggies and put the lid back on. Press "Sauté" and let the veggies cook for just 3 minutes. Put the remaining teaspoon of fat to the pot.

7. Pour a little of the sauce over them if desired. Serve and enjoy!!!

Coconut Fish Curry

Preparation Time: 6 minutes

Cooking Time: 10 minutes

Total time: 16 minutes

Servings: 5

Ingredients:

- ½ tsp. ground Turmeric
- 2 lb. (680g) Fish steaks or fillets, rinsed and cut into pieces
- 1 Tomato, chopped
- 2 ½ Green Chiles, sliced into strips ☐ 2 Medium onions, sliced into strips
- ½ tsp. Ground Fenugreek (Methi)
- 2 Garlic cloves, squeezed
- ½ tsp. ground Turmeric
- 8 Curry leaves or Bay Laurel Leaves
- 1 Tbsp. ground Coriander
- ½ tsp. ground Turmeric
- 2 tsp. ground Cumin
- 1 tsp. Chili powder, or 1 tsp. of Hot Pepper Flakes

Cooking Instructions:

1. Heat the cooker on a low heat pressure without the lid, put a little oil in the pot and then put the curry leaves and lightly fry for about a minute.

2. Put onion, garlic, and ginger and sauté until the onion is soft. Put all of the ground spices: Coriander, Cumin, Tumeric, Chili Powder and Fenugreek.

3. Sauté them together with the onions until they have released their aroma (about 2 minutes). Deglaze with the coconut milk to remove anything stuck to the pot.

4. Add the Green Chiles, Tomatoes and fish pieces. Stir to coat the fish well with the mixture. Cover the lid and cook for 7 minutes using low pressure.

5. Immediately cooking time elapses, release pressure naturally. Put salt to taste and spritz with lemon juice just before serving.

6. Serve and enjoy!!!

Sweet And Spicy Pineapple Shrimp

Preparation Time: 6 minutes

Cooking Time: 7 minutes

Total time: 13 minutes

Servings: 5

Ingredients:

- 1 Tbsp. Sambal Oelek Ground Chili Paste
- 2 Tbsp. Soy Sauce
- 1 big Red Bell Pepper cleaned and sliced
- 10 oz Calrose Rice or Quinoa
- 1.5 cups Unsweetened Pineapple Chunks drained
- 3/4 cup Unsweetened Pineapple Juice
- 1/4 cup Dry White Wine
- 2 Tbsp. Thai Sweet Chili Sauce
- 1 lb. big Shrimp, tails on frozen
- 4 Scallions chopped, White and Greens separated

Cooking Instructions:

1. Get Juice from Pineapple and keep Pineapple Chunks aside. Measure out 3/4 cup of Pineapple Juice.

2. Put Red Bell Peppers, Pineapple Juice, Wine, Chili Sauce, Soy Sauce, Sambal Oelek, Rice and chopped Scallions (the white part) to Pressure Cooker cooking pot.

3. Place frozen Shrimp on top and lock on Lid and close Pressure Valve.

4. Use high pressure to cook for 3 minutes. When the cooking time elapses, wait additional 10 minutes and then open the pot.

5. Put your pineapple Chunks and Scallion Greens and mix through.

6. Serve immediately.

Fish Tacos

Preparation Time: 6 minutes

Cooking Time: 7 minutes

Total time: 13 minutes

Servings: 5

Ingredients:

- 1-2 sprigs of fresh cilantro.
- 2 tilapia fillets
- Salt to taste
- 2 tbsp of smoked paprika
- juice of one lime
- 1 tsp of canola oil

Cooking Instructions:

1. Take a big parchment paper and put tilapia in the middle.

2. Using canola oil to sprinkle the tilapia, spray with salt and paprika, squeeze lime juice on the tilapia and sprinkle with some cilantro.

3. Bend or fold your old your parchment paper into a packet and keep no space for air ventilation. Put 1 1/2 cups of water in the bottom of your Instant Pot.

4. Place the trivet. Put the parchment packet on top of the trivet and close lid. Use high pressure and cook for 7 minutes.

5. You may cook the fish a little longer if it is thicker. Cut the fish according to how you want to place it on a taco.

6. Build your taco to your choice.

7. Serve immediately.

4 Minute Salmon, Broccoli & Potatoes

Preparation Time: 2 minutes

Cooking Time: 6 minutes

Total time: 8 minutes

Servings: 3

Ingredients:

- 70 g Broccoli
- 230 g New Potatoes
- $1^{1/2}$ Tsp Butter
- Salt & Pepper
- Fresh Herbs optional
- 7 g Salmon Fillet

Cooking Instructions:

1. Cut your broccoli into florets and put to one side. Put 150ml of water into the bottom of your Instant Pot.

2. Take up your potatoes using salt, pepper and fresh herbs to season. Also Season your salmon and broccoli with salt and pepper.

3. Put your potatoes into the steaming rack and smother them with the butter so that the butter will melt as you cook them.

4. Cover the lid on your Instant Pot and set the valve to sealing for 4 minutes on the steam function.

5. Put your broccoli florets and salmon onto the rack and cook in the same way for about 4 minutes.

6. When cooking time elapse allow natural release of pressure done. Once it has cooled down from keep warm mode you can get it out.

7. Serve and enjoy.

Salmon With Chili-Lime Sauce

Preparation Time: 7 minutes

Cooking Time: 8 minutes

Total time: 15 minutes

Calories 380 kcal

Servings: 3

Ingredients:

For steaming salmon:

- 1 tbsp olive oil
- 2 cloves garlic minced
- 2 salmon fillets 5 oz each
- 1 cup water
- 1/2 tsp paprika
- salt to taste
- Black pepper to taste (freshly ground)

For chili-lime sauce:

- 1 ½ lime juiced
- 1 1/2 tbsp honey
- 1 tbsp hot water
- 1 tbsp chopped fresh parsley
- 1/2 tsp cumin
- 1 jalapeno seeds removed and diced

Cooking Instructions:

1. Gather all the sauce ingredients and mix in a bowl and keep aside when done. Add water to the cooker and put salmon fillets on top of a steam rack inside the pot.

2. Put salt and pepper to your taste on top of the salmon fillets and season. Close and lock the lid in place.

3. Select the steam mode and adjust the cooking time to 8 minutes using high pressure. When cooking time elapses, use a quick pressure release.

4. Open the lid and transfer the salmon to a serving plate. Garnish with chili-lime sauce.

5. Serve and enjoy!!!

Savory Shrimp With Tomatoes And Feta

Preparation Time: 8 minutes

Cooking Time: 15 minutes

Total time: 23 minutes

Calories 280 kcal

Servings: 6

Ingredients:

Cook Together

- 1 tsp. oregano
- 1 tbsp. garlic
- 1.5 cups chopped onion
- 1 15 oz can tomatoes
- 1 tsp. salt
- 1/2 tsp. red pepper flakes adjust to taste
- 1 lb. frozen shrimp 21-25 count, shelled
- 2 tbsp. Butter

Add after cooking

- 1/4 cup sliced black olives
- 1 cup crumbled feta cheese
- 1/3 cup parsley

Cooking Instructions:

1. Set your Instant Pot to Sauté and put the butter when it is hot.

2. Allow it to melt a little and then put garlic and red pepper flakes, onions, tomatoes, oregano and salt. Pour the frozen shrimp.

3. Set your Instant pot to low pressure for 2 minutes. When the pot is done with the cooking time, release all pressure immediately.

4. Mix in the shrimp with all the tomato broth. Allow it to cool for a while. Pour the feta cheese, olives, and parsley on top.

5. Serve immediately.

Crustless Crab Quiche

Preparation Time: 15 minutes

Cooking Time: 53 minutes

Total time: 1 hour 8 minutes

Calories 380 kcal

Servings: 6

Ingredients:

- 1 tsp. sweet smoked paprika
- 5 eggs
- 1 cup half and half
- 10 oz. real crab meat, or a mix of crab and chopped raw shrimp
- 1 tsp. salt
- 1 tsp. pepper
- 1 tsp. Herbes de Provence
- 1 cup shredded cheese
- 1 cup chopped green onions green and white parts

Cooking Instructions:

1. Using a big bowl, mix together eggs and half-and-half with a whisk. Put salt, pepper, sweet smoked paprika, Herbes de Provence, and shredded cheese.

2. Add the chopped green onions and stir with a fork to mix completely. Put the real crab meat OR some combination of crab meat and chopped raw shrimp.

3. Spread out a sheet of aluminum foil that is cut bigger than the pan you want to use. Place the spring form pan on this sheet and crimp the sheet about the bottom.

4. Put the egg mixture into your spring form pan. Loosely close with foil or a silicone lid. Put 2 cups of water into the inner pot of your Instant Pot.

5. Place the steamer rack in the pot. Put the covered spring form pan on the trivet. Using high pressure, cook for about 50 minutes.

6. When cooking time elapses, allow the pot to rest for 10 minutes and then release all remaining pressure. Take out the hot silicone pan carefully.

7. With your knife, loosen the edges of the quiche from the pan. Remove the outer ring. Serve and enjoy!!!

VEGAN AND VEGETARIAN RECIPES

Vegan Butter Chicken with Soy Curls and Chickpeas

Preparation Time: 11 minutes

Cooking Time: 33 minutes

Total time: 44 minutes

Calories: 380 kcal

Servings: 5

Ingredients:

- ½ tsp. cayenne
- 4 big ripe tomatoes
- 3 cloves of garlic
- 1/2 inch cube of ginger
- 1 cup water
- 1 tsp. garam masala
- ½ tsp. paprika or kashmiri chili powder
- 3/4 tsp. salt
- 1 cup soy curls (dry, not rehydrated)
- 1 cup cooked chickpeas
- Cashew cream made with ¼ cup soaked cashews blended with ½ cup water
- 1/2 tsp. or more garam masala
- 1/2 tsp. or more sugar or sweetener
- 1/2 moderately hot green chile finely chopped, or use 2 tbsp finely chopped green bell pepper
- 1/2 tsp. minced or finely chopped ginger
- 1/4 cup cilantro for garnish
- 1 hot or mild green chili
- 1 tsp. kasoori methi - dried fenugreek leaves or add a 1/4 tsp ground mustard

Cooking Instructions:

1. Mix together tomatoes, garlic, ginger, chile and blend with water until smooth. Put pureed tomato mixture to the Instant pot.

2. Put soy curls, chickpeas, spices and salt. Close the lid and cook on manual for 10 minutes. Quick release after 10 minutes.

3. Set the Instant Pot on sauté and put the cashew cream, garam masala, sweetener and fenugreek leaves and mix in. Bring to a boil, taste and adjust salt, heat, sweet.

4. You may put more cayenne and salt if needed. Fold in the chopped green chile, ginger and cilantro and press cancel on the Instant pot.

5. You may also put some vegan butter or oil for additional buttery flavor.

6. Serve immediately and enjoy!!!

Maple Bourbon Sweet Potato Chili

Preparation Time: 10 minutes

Cooking Time: 23 minutes

Total time: 33 minutes

Calories: 220 kcal

Servings: 5

Ingredients:

- 4 cloves garlic minced
- 1 tbsp cooking oil
- 1 small yellow onion, thinly sliced
- 2 (14) oz cans kidney beans, drained and rinsed
- A few fresh springs of cilantro
- 4 ½ cups sweet potatoes, peeled and cut into 1/2" pieces
- 2 cups vegetable broth
- 1 ½ tbsp chili powder
- ½ tsp paprika
- 1/3 tsp cayenne pepper
- 1 (15) oz can minced tomatoes
- 1/4 cup bourbon
- 2 tbsp maple syrup
- salt and pepper, to taste
- 2 green onions, minced
- 3 small corn tortillas, toasted and sliced (optional)
- 2 tsp cumin

Cooking Instructions:

1. Set your Instant Pot to sauté, put oil, and let it heat up for 40 seconds. Put onions and heat up for about 5 minutes, stir it periodically, until onions are fragrant.

2. Put garlic and heat for another 40 seconds. Put cut sweet potatoes, chili powder, cumin, paprika, and cayenne pepper, stir until vegetables are well coated.

3. Put vegetable broth, beans, tomatoes, maple syrup, and bourbon. Cover the lid on the Instant Pot and set mode to "soup", setting the timer for 15 minutes.

4. When cooking time elapses, naturally release the pressure. Open the lid and check to make sure the sweet potatoes are tender.

5. If you are making use of tortillas, lightly oil a cast iron skillet and pan fry the tortillas on each side for 3 minutes.

6. Take it out from heat and let cool before cutting into thin strips. You may add these optional toppings: cilantro, green onions, and toasted tortillas.

7. Serve and enjoy.

Easy Vegan Mashed Potatoes

Preparation Time: 8 minutes

Cooking Time: 23 minutes

Total time: 31 minutes

Calories: 90 kcal

Servings: 5

Ingredients:

- 5 cloves of garlic
- 6 potatoes cubed into large pieces Yukon gold
- 1/2 tsp salt
- 1 ½ tbsp extra virgin olive oil or vegan butter
- dash of parlsey or thyme
- pinch of nutmeg
- 1 cup full fat coconut milk
- fresh chives for garnish
- a good dash of black pepper

Cooking Instructions:

1. Gather and cook the cubed potatoes, garlic cloves, 1/4 tsp salt with 1.5 cups water using high pressure for 4 minutes in Instant.

2. Release the pressure after 5 minutes. Add the potatoes into a large pot, adding enough water to cover them.

3. Bring to a boil and simmer for about 15 minutes, until they are soft. Remove them to a colander to drain very well.

4. Transfer to a bowl, let sit for a few minutes to dry out. Mash lightly and let sit for a minute for the steam to escape. Mash the cooked garlic.

5. Put salt and the rest of the ingredients and half cup coconut milk. Mix and whip lightly, just enough to add air and still have some texture.

6. Allow to rest for a minute for the milks to incorporate and absorb. Put 1/3 tsp or more salt as needed. Put more coconut milk to be creamier if needed and mix.

7. Put 2 tbsp nutritional yeast for cheesy potatoes. Garnish with chives.

8. Serve and enjoy.

Walnut Lentil Tacos

Preparation Time: 5 minutes

Cooking Time: 10 minutes

Total time: 15 minutes

Yield: 11-12 tacos

Ingredients:

- 1/2 tsp. garlic powder
- 1 white onion, diced
- 1 ½ tbsp. olive oil
- 1 cup dried brown lentils
- 2 garlic clove, minced
- 1 tbsp. chili powder
- 1/4 tsp. onion powder
- 1/3 tsp. red pepper flakes
- 1 ½ tsp. ground cumin
- 1/2 tsp. kosher salt
- 1/3 tsp. freshly ground pepper
- 2 ½ cups vegetable broth
- 1/2 tsp. paprika
- 1 14 oz, can fire-roasted diced tomatoes
- 3/4 cup chopped walnuts
- 1/3 tsp. oregano

Taco toppings of choice: shredded lettuce, tomato, jalapenos, Flour or corn tortillas

Cooking Instructions:

1. Switch the Instant Pot on and press the Sauté button. Put the olive oil, onion and garlic clove and sauté until onion cooked through.

2. Stir occasionally for about 4 minutes. Put the spices and stir together. press cancel and put the vegetable broth, tomatoes, walnuts and lentils and stir to mix well.

3. Put the top on and cook on high manual pressure for 10 minutes. Allow pressure come down naturally for 4 minutes and do quick release.

4. Open the lid and stir lentils, seasoning to taste if needed. You may add toppings of your choice.

5. Serve immediately.

Cilantro Lime Quinoa

Preparation Time: 6 minutes

Cooking Time: 10 minutes

Total time: 16 minutes

Calories 97 kcal

Servings: 5

Ingredients:

- 2 Tbsp. lime juice
- 1 cup quinoa rinsed and drained (any color)
- salt to taste
- zest of one lime
- 1/2 cup chopped cilantro
- 1 ¼ cups vegetable broth

Cooking Instructions:

1. Put the quinoa and 1 1/4 cup vegetable broth to the Instant Pot.

2. Close and lock the lid in place. Select Manual, High Pressure for 5 minutes. When cooking time elapses, allow the pressure to release naturally.

3. Carefully open the lid and pour the lime juice, lime zest, and cilantro. Taste and add salt to taste.

4. Serve and enjoy!!!

Vegan Lentil Chili

Preparation Time: 10 minutes

Cooking Time: 22 minutes

Total time: 32 minutes

Servings: 5

Ingredients:

- 1 tsp. dried oregano
- 1 onion, chopped
- 4 cloves minced garlic
- 2 carrots, chopped
- 2 jalapeños, chopped
- 1 1/2 tbsp. chili powder
- 1/2 tsp. ground coriander
- 1/2 tsp. salt
- 1/2 cup chopped fresh cilantro
- 1 14 oz. can crushed tomatoes
- 1 30 oz. can fire roasted diced tomatoes
- 1 tbsp. olive oil
- 2 cups brown or green lentils.
- 4 ½ cups vegetable broth
- 1 tsp. fresh lime juice
- 1 tbsp. cumin

Cooking Instructions:

1. Put olive oil in the Instant Pot, hit the sauté button on the Instant Pot and heat the oil for sometimes.

2. Put the onion, garlic, carrots and jalapeños and heat until soft, about 4 minutes.

3. Put the spices and remaining ingredients except for lime juice and cilantro, and then close.

4. Cook on high pressure for 15 minutes, and then do quick-release.

5. Pour lime juice and cilantro

6. Serve immediately.

Mushroom Risotto

Preparation Time: 12 minutes

Cooking Time: 20 minutes

Total time: 32 minutes

Calories: 370 kcal

Servings: 5

Ingredients:

- 1 ½ tbsp olive oil
- 2 ½ tbsp vegan butter, divided
- 1 medium onion, diced
- 4 cloves garlic, minced
- 10 oz cremini mushrooms dry brushed & minced
- 3/4 tsp dried thyme
- 1 ½ cups arborio rice
- 1/2 cup dry white wine
- 4 cups vegetable broth, low sodium
- 1 ¼ tsp sea salt, more to taste
- Fresh ground pepper to taste
- 1 cup frozen peas, thawed
- 4 tbsp Vegan Parmesan Cheese (optional)

Cooking Instructions:

1. Switch on the Sauté mode of your Instant Pot and put the oil and butter. Heat the oil; put the onions and sauté about 3 minutes.

2. Put the garlic and thyme and sauté for a minute. You can now put the mushrooms and sauté for about 4 minutes until soft. Put the rice and stir to coat well.

3. Pour the wine and cook until the liquid mostly cooks down. About 2 minutes. Now, pour the broth, salt, and pepper then close and secure the lid.

4. Set the steam release handle to the Sealing position. Cancel the Sauté function and push the Pressure Cooker (Manual Setting) button to high pressure.

5. Set the time to 6 minutes. When the Instant Pot has come to pressure, you'll see the 6 minutes displayed on the screen again.

6. When the cooking time elapses, carefully set the steam release handle to the Venting position for a quick release.

7. Open the lid immediately the float valve goes down. Note, the risotto will look soupy when you first remove the lid. Just stir for sometimes and it will thicken up.

8. Put the peas, butter, and vegan parmesan. Top with fresh-cut parsley, crushed red pepper flakes, and fresh cracked pepper.

9. Serve and enjoy!!!

Potato Curry

Preparation Time: 12 minutes

Cooking Time: 45 minutes

Total time: 57 minutes

Calories: 270 kcal

Servings: 5

Ingredients:

- 1 420ml can coconut milk, full fat or light
- 1 medium yellow onion, chopped
- 4 large cloves of garlic, chopped finely
- 950g / about 5 heaping cups baby potatoes
- 2 tbsp curry powder or curry paste
- 500mls / around 2 cups water
- 3 tbsp arrowroot powder.
- 1 tbsp sugar
- Salt and pepper to taste
- 1 tsp chili pepper flakes or a small fresh chili chopped
- 400g / 2 heaping cups fresh green beans, chopped into small sizes

Cooking Instructions:

1. Turn your instant pot to sauté mode. When it is hot, put a few drops of water and cook the onions until soft. Put the garlic and cook for one minute.

2. Press the keep warm/cancel button. Put everything else to the Instant Pot except the green beans and arrowroot.

3. Set your Instant Pot to 20 minutes on manual using high pressure and allow the pressure to release naturally after this time.

4. Press keep warm/cancel remove the lid and press SAUTE. Put the arrowroot into a small bowl and pour a few tbsp of water to make it thick.

5. Pour it into the Instant Pot stirring as you go. Put salt and pepper to taste then add the green beans and cook for about 5 minutes until they are soft.

6. Serve immediately and enjoy!!!

Carrot Ginger Soup

Preparation Time: 15 minutes

Cooking Time: 17 minutes

Total time: 32 minutes

Calories: 270 kcal

Servings: 5

Ingredients:

- 2 tbsp. grapeseed oil or preferred oil
- 1 medium onion, diced
- 4 cloves garlic, minced
- 1.5 tbsp. fresh ginger, grated
- 1 tsp. dried thyme
- 1/2 tsp. ground coriander
- 1/2 tsp. crushed red pepper
- 2 bay leaves
- 2 lb. carrots (about 6 large), rough chopped
- 4 cups vegetable broth, low sodium
- 1 tsp. sea salt, more to taste
- Fresh cracked pepper to taste (optional)
- 1 cup canned coconut milk, full-fat
- 1-2 tbsp. lime juice (sub lemon)

Cooking Instructions:

1. Switch on the sauté mode of your Instant Pot and add the oil. When the oil is heated, put the onions and sauté for about 3 minutes.

2. Put the garlic and ginger, sauté for 2 minutes. Put thyme, coriander and crushed red pepper. Sauté for 50 seconds.

3. Cancel the sauté function and put the broth, carrots, bay leaves, salt, and cracked pepper. Cover the lid and set the steam release handle to the Sealing position.

4. Keep the Pressure Cooker (Manual Setting) button to high pressure and set the time to 6 minutes.

5. Upon the end of the cooking time, don't touch anything, allow the pressure naturally release for 3 minutes.

6. Set the steam release handle to the Venting position, immediately the float Valve goes down you can carefully open the lid.

7. Take out the bay leaves and put the coconut milk and lime juice. Using a regular blender, blend until smooth.

8. Taste for seasoning and put more if you desire. If for any reason, the soup is too thick for your taste, you can add a small amount of vegetable broth to thin it out.

9. Serve immediately.

APPETIZER RECIPES

Prosciutto-wrapped Asparagus Canes

Preparation Time: 5 minutes

Cooking Time: 7 minutes

Total time: 12 minutes

Servings: 5

Ingredients:

- 1lb (480g) thick Asparagus
- 8oz (235g) thinly sliced Prosciutto

Cooking Instructions:

1. Arrange the pressure cooker by adding the minimum amount of water (1 to 2 cups) and keep aside. Take the asparagus spears and wrap in prosciutto.

2. Keep any extra un-wrapped spears in a single layer on the bottom of the steamer basket. Put the prosciutto-wrapped asparagus on top in a single layer also.

3. Keep the basket inside the pressure cooker and close the lid. Switch the heat up high and when the pan reaches pressure.

4. Lower the heat and count about 3 minutes cooking time at high pressure. When cooking time elapses, open the pressure cooker and do natural release.

5. Get the steamer basket out immediately and place the asparagus on a serving platter so they may not be gradually cooked by remaining heat.

6. Serve immediately!!!

Black Bean Dip

Preparation Time: 20 minutes

Cooking Time: 33 minutes

Total time: 53 minutes

Servings: 25

Ingredients:

- 1 medium onion, diced
- 3 cloves of garlic, peeled + minced
- 2 medium jalapeños (approx. 1/3 cup chopped)
- 1 ½ cup vegetable broth
- 1 ½ tbsp avocado oil
- juice of 1 lime
- chopped tomatoes, sliced jalapeños, diced bell pepper, chopped red onion, cilantro, sour cream for toppings
- 2 tsp ground cumin
- 1 tsp smoked paprika
- 3/4 tsp sea salt
- 1 ½ cup dried black beans
- 1/2 tsp chili powder
- 1/2 tsp ground coriander
- 1 (15 oz) can diced or crushed tomatoes

Cooking Instructions:

1. Wash your black beans and put them in your Instant Pot. Dice and chop your veggies and mince your garlic.

2. Put veggies, garlic, tomatoes, broth, oil, lime juice, and spices to the pot and mix. Press the bean button and cook for about 25 minutes using high pressure.

3. Allow a natural release for 10 minutes, then do quick release on remaining pressure. Using a blender or food processor, blend the tip all together.

4. You can add more spice either from hot sauce, spicy salsa, red pepper flakes, or cayenne to the mix and add any extra spices/salt to suit your tastes.

5. Serve and enjoy!

Cocktail Meatballs

Preparation Time: 5 minutes

Cooking Time: 7 minutes

Total time: 12 minutes

Serves: 65 pieces

Ingredients:

- 1 tbsp. minced garlic
- 2 lb. cooked Perfect Homestyle Meatballs
- 1/4 cup honey
- 1/2 cup ketchup ☐ 2 tbsp soy sauce
- 1/3 cup brown sugar
- garnish with sliced green onions (optional)

Cooking Instructions:

1. Mix brown sugar, honey, ketchup, soy sauce, and garlic in pressure cooker.

2. Set to sauté mode and stir to mix properly. When the mixture comes to a boil, put the frozen fully cooked meatballs.

3. Close the lid and set to high pressure for 5 minutes. Allow to naturally release pressure when cooking time elapse.

4. Serve hot and enjoy!

Buffalo Ranch Chicken Dip

Preparation Time: 5 minutes

Cooking Time: 20 minutes

Total time: 25 minutes

Calories 506 kcal

Servings: 6

Ingredients:

- 1 ½ lb. chicken breast
- 1 packet ranch dip
- 1 ½ cup Hot Sauce
- 1 stick butter
- 15 oz cheddar cheese
- 8 oz cream cheese

Cooking Instructions:

1. Put chicken, cream cheese, butter, hot sauce, and a packet of Ranch dip in your Instant Pot.

2. Using manual settings, cook on high pressure for 15 minutes and do a quick Release.

3. Cut your chicken with fork or use your mixer to break it up and pour in cheddar cheese.

4. Serve and enjoy.

Cranberry Pecan Brie

Preparation Time: 15 minutes

Cooking Time: 30 minutes

Total time: 45 minutes

Servings: 4

Ingredients:

- 1 (8-oz) round of Brie
- 1/4 cup cranberry jalapeno preserves
- 3 tbsp. candied pecans
- 1 tsp. minced fresh thyme

Cooking Instructions:

1. Slice through the rind on top of the Brie in a grid pattern. Put the Brie in a baking dish in a way it will fit in your pressure cooking pot.

2. Cover baking dish tightly with foil. Construct a foil sling for lifting the baking dish out of the pressure cooker by taking an 18" strip of foil and folding it twice.

3. Put 1 cup of water into the pressure cooker and place the rack in the bottom. Keep the baking dish on center of the foil strip.

4. Lower it into the pressure cooker on to the rack. Fold the foil strips down so they may not disturb you when closing the lid.

5. Close the lid, select high pressure and set the time for 20 minutes. When cooking time elapses, use a quick pressure release.

6. Carefully remove lid when valve drops. You can now inspect to make sure cheese is melted and piping hot.

7. Scoop to a serving plate and top with preserves, pecans and thyme.

8. Serve immediately.

Beer-Braised Pulled Ham

Preparation Time: 15 minutes

Cooking Time: 30 minutes

Total time: 45 minutes

Servings: 14

Ingredients:

- 1/2 tsp. coarsely ground pepper
- 2 bottles (12 oz each) beer or nonalcoholic beer
- 3/4 cup German or Dijon mustard, divided
- 1 fully cooked bone-in ham (4 lb.)
- 16 pretzel hamburger buns, split
- Dill pickle slices (optional)
- 4 fresh rosemary sprigs

Cooking Instructions:

1. Whisk together beer, 1/2 cup mustard and pepper into your Instant Pot. Put ham and rosemary, close lid and make sure vent is closed.

2. Using manual setting, keep the cooker on high pressure and set time to 20 minutes. When cooking time elapses, allow pressure to naturally release for 15 minutes, do a quick release any remaining pressure.

3. Take out ham and allow it to cool. Discard rosemary sprigs. Skim fat from liquid remaining in pressure cooker.

4. Select sauté mode and set on high pressure. Bring liquid to a boil; cook for 7 minutes. Hand-touch the ham.

5. When it is cool enough to handle, cut meat with two forks. Put back ham to pressure cooker; heat through.

6. Serve and enjoy!!!

Mini Teriyaki Turkey Sandwiches

Preparation Time: 15 minutes

Cooking Time: 30 minutes

Total time: 45 minutes

Servings: 24

Ingredients:

- 2 tbsp. cornstarch
- 2/3 cup packed brown sugar
- 2/3 cup reduced-sodium soy sauce
- 1/3 cup cider vinegar
- 4 garlic cloves, minced
- 1 tbsp. minced fresh gingerroot
- 1 1/2 tsp. pepper
- 2 tbsp. butter, melted
- 2 tbsp. cold water
- 20 Hawaiian sweet rolls
- 2 boneless skinless turkey breast halves (2 ½ lbs. each)

Cooking Instructions:

1. Put turkey into your Instant Pot. Using a small container, mix the ingredients; pour over turkey. Lock lid; make sure vent is closed.

2. Select manual setting and set time for 25 minutes on high pressure. When cooking time elapses, allow pressure to naturally release for 15 minutes, then quick release any remaining pressure.

3. Get turkey out from pressure cooker. Select sauté mode and set on high pressure. Boil the juices. Using a small container, mix cornstarch and water until smooth; gradually pour into cooking juices.

4. Cook and stir for 3 minutes. When it is cool enough to handle, cut meat with two forks, return meat to Instant Pot and stir while you heat through.

5. Heat the Instant Pot. Open and split rolls, brush cut sides with butter. Place on an ungreased baking sheet, cut side up. Bake until golden brown for about 10 minutes.

6. Spoon 1/3 cup turkey mixture on roll bottoms.

7. Serve and enjoy!

Cuban Pulled Pork Sandwiches

Preparation Time: 15 minutes

Cooking Time: 30 minutes

Total time: 45 minutes

Servings: 15

Ingredients:

- 12 garlic cloves, minced
- 2 tsp. salt
- 2 tsp. pepper
- 1 tbsp. olive oil
- 1 cup orange juice
- 2 tbsp. spiced rum, optional
- 2 tbsp. ground coriander
- 2 tsp. white pepper
- 1 tsp. cayenne pepper
- 1/2 cup lime juice
- 1 boneless pork shoulder butt roast (5 lbs.)

Sandwiches:

- 1 1/2 lbs. Swiss cheese, sliced
- 2 loaves (1 lb. each) French bread
- Yellow mustard, optional
- 16 dill pickle slices
- 1 1/2 lbs. thinly sliced deli ham

Cooking instructions:

1. Divide pork into 2 pieces, season with salt and pepper. Select sauté mode on your Instant Pot using high pressure.

2. Add oil; working in batches, fry pork to become brown on all sides and remove from cooker. Put orange and lime juices, stirring to scrape browned bits from bottom of cooker.

3. Put garlic, rum, if desired, coriander, white pepper and cayenne pepper. Return pork and any collected juices to cooker. Close lid and make sure vent is closed.

4. Select manual setting; using high pressure and set cooking time for 20 minutes. When cooking time elapses, naturally release pressure for 8 minutes, then quick release any remaining pressure.

5. Take out roast; when cool enough to handle, cut with two forks and get 1 cup cooking liquid from cooker, put to pork and toss.

6. Divide each loaf of bread in half lengthwise. You may spread mustard over cut sides of bread if you desire.

7. Layer bottom halves of bread with pickles, pork, ham and cheese.

8. Serve and enjoy!!!

DESSERT RECIPES

Apple Bread with Salted Caramel Icing

Preparation Time: 20 minutes

Cooking Time: 1 hour 15 minutes

Total time: 1 hour 35 minutes

Calories: 545 kcal

Servings: 12

Ingredients:

- 4 cups apples Peeled Cored, and cubed
- 1 cup sugar
- 3 eggs
- 1 tbsp vanilla
- 1 tbsp apple pie spice
- 2 ½ cups flour
- 1 stick butter
- 1 tbsp baking powder

For the topping:

- 1 stick salted butter
- 2 cups brown sugar
- 1 cup heavy cream
- 2 cups powdered sugar

Cooking Instructions:

1. Using your mixer, mix together eggs, butter, apple pie spice, and sugar until creamy and smooth. Put your apples.

2. Use another bowl and mix flour and baking powder. Add your flour mix to your wet mix. If the batter was thick. Pour into your 7" springform pan.

3. Keep your trivet in the bottom of your Instant pot and one cup of water. Keep your pan on the trivet and set the Instant Pot on manual high pressure for 72 minutes.

4. When cooking time elapses, allow natural pressure to release then do a quick release. You can now remove and top with Icing.

5. Serve and enjoy!

Apple Crisp

Preparation Time: 6 minutes

Cooking Time: 8 minutes

Total time: 14 minutes

Servings: 5

Ingredients:

- 2 ½ tsp. cinnamon
- 1/2 tsp. nutmeg
- 1/2 cup water
- 1 tbsp. maple syrup
- 4 1/2 tbsp. butter
- 3/4 cup old fashioned rolled oats
- 1/4 cup flour
- 1/4 cup brown sugar
- 5 medium sized apples, peeled and chopped into chunks
- 1/2 tsp. salt

Cooking Instructions:

1. Put apples on the bottom of your Instant Pot. Pour in cinnamon and nutmeg. Top with water and maple syrup.

2. Heat the butter to melt. Using a small bowl, mix together melted butter, oats, flour, brown sugar and salt. You can drop by the spoonful on top of the apples.

3. Close the lid on the instant pot. Use the manual setting, and cook on high pressure for 10 minutes.

4. Use a natural release and allow it to rest for a few minutes to make the sauce thickened.

5. Put your toppings like vanilla ice cream.

6. Serve and enjoy!!!

Mini-Lemon Cheesecakes

Preparation Time: 8 minutes

Cooking Time: 8 minutes

Total time: 16 minutes

Servings: 5

Ingredients:

- ½ tsp. vanilla
- 6 half pint mason jars
- 18 oz. cream cheese, room temp
- ½ cup sugar
- 1.5 cups water
- 1 tsp. flour
- ¼ cup sour cream, room temp
- 1 tbsp. Lemon Juice
- zest of one lemon
- 3 eggs, room temp
- 1 jar lemon curd (found in the jam & jelly aisle)
- Raspberries (optional)

Cooking Instructions:

1. Using a big mixing container, beat together cream cheese, sugar, and flour until mixture is creamy with no lumps.

2. Pour in vanilla, sour cream, lemon juice, and lemon zest just until mixed well. Beat in one egg at a time just until mixed. You may not need to overbeat.

3. Take each jar and filled with ¼ cup of cheesecake batter. Gently drop 1tbsp of lemon curd on top of batter.

4. Put an additional ¼ cup cheesecake batter to each jar on top of the lemon curd and cover each jar with foil in a loose way.

5. Put 1.5 cups of water to the bottom of the Instant Pot. Keep the trivet on the bottom. Line up three jars on top of the trivet.

6. Stack the other three jars on the first three. Close the lid to the Instant Pot and set the vent is in the pressure cooking position.

7. Using manual settings, cook on high pressure for 8 minutes. When the cooking time elapses, do a natural pressure release for at least 10 minutes.

8. Using a towel, carefully remove the jars from the Instant Pot, and allow it to cool and store in the refrigerator until ready to serve.

9. Garnish with additional lemon curd and raspberries.

10. Serve and enjoy!!!

Berries And Cream Breakfast Cake

Preparation Time: 8 minutes

Cooking Time: 10 minutes

Total time: 18 minutes

Servings: 5

Ingredients:

Breakfast Cake

- 2 tsp. vanilla extract
- 6 eggs
- 1/3 cup sugar
- Sweet Yogurt Glaze
- 2 tbsp. butter, melted
- 3/4 cup ricotta cheese
- 3/4 cup plain or vanilla yogurt
- 1/2 tsp. salt
- 2 tsp. baking powder
- 1/2 cup Berry Compote
- Berry Compote (prepare and chill beforehand)
- 1 cup whole wheat pastry flour or white whole wheat flour

Sweet Yogurt Glaze

- 1/4 cup yogurt
- 1/2 tsp. vanilla extract
- 1 tsp. milk
- 1-2 tbsp. powdered sugar

Cooking Instructions:

1. Make the Berry Compote beforehand first so it is cold and thick because if used warm, it has a tendency to sink to the bottom of the pan.

2. For the Breakfast Cake, generously grease a 6 cup Bundt pan with nonstick cooking spray. Mix together the eggs and sugar until smooth.

3. Put the butter, ricotta cheese, yogurt, and vanilla and mix until smooth. Using a different container, whisk together the flour, salt, and baking powder.

4. Combine with the egg mixture. Pour into the prepared bundt pan. With a half cup of Berry Compote, drop by tbsp on top of the batter and swirl in with a knife.

5. Put a cup of water to the pressure cooker pot and place a trivet inside. Keep the bundt pan on the trivet.

6. Close the lid and turn pressure release knob to a sealed position. Cook at high pressure for 30 minutes.

7. Prepare the Sweet Yogurt Glaze while the cake is cooking by whisking together the yogurt, vanilla, milk, and powdered sugar; keep aside.

8. When cooking elapses, allow a natural release for 10 minutes and then release any remaining pressure.

9. Take out pan from pressure cooker. Allow it to cool. Loosen the sides of the cake from the pan and gently turn over onto a plate.

10. Serve warm and enjoy.

Apple And Ricotta Cake

Preparation Time: 8 minutes

Cooking Time: 22 minutes

Total time: 30 minutes

Servings: 7

Ingredients:

- 2 cups water
- 2 apples, 1 sliced 1 diced
- 1 tbsp. lemon juice
- ¼ cup raw sugar
- 2 eggs
- 1 cup ricotta cheese
- ⅓ cup sugar
- 3 tbsp. extra-virgin olive oil
- 1 tsp. vanilla extract
- 1 cup all-purpose flour
- ⅛ tsp. cinnamon
- 2 tsp. baking powder
- 1 tsp. baking soda

Cooking Instructions:

1. Put water to the base of pressure cooker, plus steamer basket and keep aside. Slice one apple and mince the other and cover with lemon juice.

2. Make a shallow and wide 4-cup capacity heat-proof bowl by adding a disk of wax paper at the bottom, oiling and dusting all the inside with flour.

3. Spray the base of the bowl with raw sugar and arrange the sliced apples in the bowl. Using a small mixing container, mix the egg, ricotta, sugar, olive oil and vanilla using a fork.

4. Then, spray the flour, cinnamon, baking powder and baking soda in the mixing container using a flour sifter.

5. Using a regular blender, blend well with a fork and then put the apple dices. Pour into prepared bowl and lower into the pressure cooker without covering.

6. Cover the lid, set the valve to pressure cooking position and cook for 25 minutes at high pressure. When cooking time elapses, open the pressure cooker with the natural pressure release.

7. Unplug the cooker, and open the lid when the pressure indicator/lid-lock has gone down about 30 minutes.

8. Remove the cooker off the burner and wait for the pressure to come down on its own about 10 minutes.

9. Taste if the cake is done by inserting a toothpick in the middle - if it comes out dirty lower back into the pressure and cook for a few more minutes.

10. Take the cake out onto a serving plate.

11. Serve and enjoy!!!

Applesauce

Preparation Time: 3 minutes

Cooking Time: 9 minutes

Total time: 12 minutes

Calories: 140 kcal

Servings: 5

Ingredients:

- 1 cup water
- 1-2 drops cinnamon essential oil
- 1 tsp organic cinnamon optional
- 6-8 medium to large apples Granny Smith, Gala, McIntosh, Fuji, etc.

Cooking Instructions:

1. Slice apples into 2-inch chunks. Throw away the core, stem and seeds. Put them in Instant Pot along with 1 cup of water.

2. Close Instant Pot lid and set to manual high pressure for 9 minutes making sure the steam vent is sealed.

3. The Instant Pot will take about 8 minutes to reach high pressure, and then will cook for 8 minutes. When cooking time elapses, allow it to rest for about 3 minutes.

4. Turn steam vent to release pressure. You may open the lid when all steam has evaporated. With immersion blender, blend to smooth out applesauce to your taste.

5. Put 2 drops of cinnamon oil or powder to taste. Allow it to cool or put in the refrigerator.

6. Serve and enjoy!!!

Homemade Pumpkin Puree

Preparation Time: 5 minutes

Cooking Time: 14 minutes

Total time: 19 minutes

Servings: 5

Ingredients:

- 4 lbs. pie pumpkin
- 1 cup water

Cooking Instructions:

1. Get out the stem from the pumpkin. Put a steamer basket in the bottom of the pressure cooker and put 1 cup of water.

2. Put the pumpkin on the basket cover the lid without touching the top of the pumpkin. Close the pressure cooker and cook on high pressure for 15 minutes.

3. Allow the pressure naturally release. Take out the pumpkin from the pressure cooker (use the handles of the rack) and place on a cutting board.

4. Allow it to cool until it is easy to handle. Cut the pumpkin in half, take out the seeds, goop, and peel off the skin.

5. Using a regular blender, blend the soft pumpkin until smooth and add a tbsp of water, if needed to help it along.

6. Serve and enjoy!!!